A Culinary History of the

CHESAPEAKE
BAY

A Culinary History of the
CHESAPEAKE BAY

FOUR CENTURIES OF FOOD & RECIPES

·TANGIE HOLIFIELD·

AMERICAN PALATE

Published by American Palate
A Division of The History Press
Charleston, SC
www.historypress.com

First published 2021

Manufactured in the United States

ISBN 9781467142137

Library of Congress Control Number: 2021943421

In Loving Memory of My Mother,
Janie A. Holifield

Contents

CONTENTS

Acknowledgements

Giving thanks to the Creator and to my ancestors for granting me the gifts and the ability to pursue the writing of this book, for I am truly grateful beyond the measure of time and space of simply existing.

I have been carrying this notion of a cookbook in my head for almost fifteen years now. Turning an idea into a book is as difficult as it sounds. And yet the experience has been both challenging and rewarding. It should be noted that the vision of this cookbook was supported by so many people who provided their guidance, time, talents and insights to make this work a reality.

This book would not have been made possible without the support and inspiration of my family. Food has always been my passion, and that was instilled in me at an early age by my grandmother Mrs. Jennie Adams. And even though she is no longer among the living, I still feel her presence around me and surrounding our extended family, as her spirit still guides all of us in love. To my family, thank you for always being there to light the way, especially my mother, father and brother, who provided that extra love and support even in the darkest of times when I doubted myself. To my friends, a special thanks for supporting me in all of my culinary endeavors and for providing honest critiques on my social media pages and being food tasters.

I would like to Emilie Sandoz-Voyer, senior special projects editor at Girl Friday Productions, for her editorial work in assisting me in preparing the original book proposal that led to the development of this cookbook.

Special thanks to Kate Jenkins, the ever-patient acquisitions manager, her editorial board and her amazing team of experts at The History Press who worked their "magic" in bringing this project to life. I do not believe I could have completed this work without her guidance, patience and encouragement.

To all the librarians, curators, digital media managers, historical societies and museums, thank you for providing the permissions and access to the collections of artwork and original source materials that help make the history of this work come alive. Special thanks to Emily Flint (University of Maryland), Tom Lisanti (New York Public Library), Katelyn Kean (Chesapeake Bay Maritime Museum), Alexandra C. Lane (The White House Historical Association), Conna Clark (Philadelphia Museum of Art), the Art Institute of Chicago, the Wye House Plantation, the Library of Congress, Delaware Historical Society, the Maryland State Archives, the Maryland Historical Society, the Baltimore American Indian Center and Museum and the Reginald F. Lewis Museum.

Last but not least, thank you to India Jackson at Flaunt Your Fire and Erica Courdae of Silver Immersions and the members at Pause on the Play for making me put my best foot forward in presenting myself and creating a brand as this book makes its debut into the world.

The Awakening Land

Throughout human history, arable land, the flow of water and climatic factors have been the most important pillars in the evolution of agriculture, as well as sustaining human beings and the society that is created around the natural environment.

The Fertile Crescent, also known as the "cradle of civilization," is a sickle-shaped region where agriculture and early human civilizations like the Sumer and ancient Egypt flourished due to inundations from the surrounding Nile, Euphrates and Tigris Rivers. Within the region, agricultural and technological advances led to the use of irrigation. It should be noted that the most successful civilizations in history have lived near rivers and maintained healthy soils so that food production was sustainable for a growing population. The very same can be said for the Mid-Atlantic coast of the United States, where the climate and geography of this region affected all aspects of human development.

CLIMATE

Geologically speaking, the Atlantic slope of North America was shaped by many tectonic, volcanic and glacial events that created a diverse geology, interesting landforms and topographic elevations that range from sea level to 3,800 feet. The region receives thirty-six to fifty inches of precipitation annually. This, in turn, creates a diversity of wetlands and aquatic systems, like Maryland's Eastern Shore.

The temperate, mid-continental climate of the area also contributed to the farming potential since the time of the Indigenous tribes settling in the region. The region has four distinct seasons, with temperatures being moderated by the Chesapeake Bay and the Atlantic Ocean, producing an annual climate pattern more typical of southern locations, with cool, wet winters and warm, humid summers. The average monthly temperature ranges from 26.9 to 44 degrees Fahrenheit in winter months. Hurricanes and nor'easters during the winter months affect the region and have increased with intensity and frequency in the past decade. During the summer months, temperatures range from 76.9 to 85 degrees Fahrenheit.

Geography

When most people think of geography, or the lay of the land, few will think about the underlying soil. Even when the average person looks at the soil, all they will see is the "dirt" beneath their feet. But soil is so much more than that. We must be mindful that soil is a precious natural resource that we take for granted all too often. Soils, no matter where they are found in the world, are a mixture of rocks and minerals, organic matter, air, water and living things. In addition to serving as a habitat for all living creatures and a foundation for the buildings and structures that we build, the soil is also the foundation for the crops we grow and eat for sustenance.

The soils across the Mid-Atlantic Coastal Plain, including the Chesapeake region, are rich, contributing to the abundance of flora and fauna found throughout the region. These soils are also as diverse as the people who cultivated them for agriculture. Since the healthiest soils produce the most food, these soils have also been at the center of the cultural and economic development of Mid-Atlantic foodways and cuisine. Geographically speaking, the area can be divided into three distinct physiographic regions: 1) the Mid-Atlantic Coastal Plain; 2) the Chesapeake Bay Lowlands; and 3) Lower New England–Northern Piedmont. If the Appalachian Mountains and coastal lowlands were not present, there would probably be fewer ranges for animals to roam and fewer fertile lands to grow crops that sustained the original Indigenous populations. Over the centuries, the Mid-Atlantic region has become one of the most highly populated areas in the country, with many cities that are continuously extending outward into the region and beyond the rural boundaries. Today, arable land for farming is becoming increasingly fragmented by first- and second-home development. While the mountainous areas of the Mid-Atlantic region are lightly settled, the valleys have long been developed for agriculture. Both are rapidly succumbing to development pressures, changing agricultural production and affecting how and what we eat in these modern times.

Plants and Animals

Before the arrival of European colonists, the Mid-Atlantic regional natural vegetation was quite different from what it is today. For example, prior to the establishment of European settlements in 1634, about nine-tenths of Maryland was forested. For nearly four hundred years, the region of the Chesapeake Bay changed significantly as human activities felled forests, cleared the land and plowed and urbanized the landscape. By the early twenty-first century, only some two-fifths of the state remained forested. On the western shore of the Chesapeake Bay, the typical upland forest is dominated by American beech, white oak, tulip poplar and hickory, with red maple increasingly abundant. Drier upland forests feature oaks and sometimes hickory, with dogwood, arrowwood and laurel found in the sub-canopy layer and chokeberries, huckleberries and blueberries ubiquitous throughout. Early successional stands on dry uplands are often dominated by Virginia pine. The extensive floodplain and slope-bottom habitats on the western shore also support sweet gum, red maple and tulip poplar, with sycamore, birch and ironwood common along riparian edges.

To the east, in uplands on the Delmarva Peninsula, native species loblolly pine forests—both natural and planted—predominate, with an abundance of southern red oak, white oak and willow oak, hickory, red maple and American holly. Virginia pine also typically dominates dry upland habitats, especially lands that are recovering from disturbance. In lower, wetter areas, red maple and sweet gum are more abundant, along with black gum, but loblolly pine and American holly remain in areas where flooding is seasonal. Highbush blueberries and sweet pepperbush dominate the shrub layer, while sweetbay magnolia reaches into the sub-canopy. Black gum and green ash become common in tidally influenced swamps on Delmarva, and some areas contain sizable stands of Atlantic white cedar.

The dominant fauna in the region includes deer; small mammals such as rabbit, squirrel, muskrat and fox; and birds such as turkey and waterfowl. Common reptiles and amphibians include diamondback terrapins, loggerhead turtles, snakes, frogs, toads, salamanders and newts. Many of the aquatic reptiles and amphibians common in the Mid-Atlantic are likely more abundant in the Bay than in adjacent Piedmont areas, simply because of the greater abundance of wetland habitats.

The Chesapeake Bay Watershed constitutes the largest estuary in the United States. It extends north/east/west into seven adjoining states: Maryland, Virginia, West Virginia, Delaware, Pennsylvania, New Jersey and New York state, plus the federal capital city of Washington in the District of Columbia. Due to the fact that over fifty major tributaries feed into the Bay as fresh water and an approximately equal portion of water enters from the Atlantic Ocean as salt water, all the waterways connected to the Chesapeake Bay are brackish. Given the predominance of the Chesapeake Bay and numerous major tidal rivers, avian species characteristic of the region include bald eagles, osprey, Canada geese, great blue herons, many species of diving and dabbling ducks, gulls and other shorebirds. The Chesapeake region also has an abundance of aquatic fauna, and these regularly include oysters, clams, blue crabs, perch, striped bass, herring, shad, alewife and sturgeon. During the warm season, bluefish, weakfish, croaker, menhaden, flounder and spot are found in the coastal waters of the Mid-Atlantic. It should also be noted that all of the vertebrates found in Delaware probably also occur in Maryland, while a few more typically southern species are found in the Virginia portion of the ecoregion.

The vast abundance of plant and animal species had a significant contribution to the development of the food pathways in the Mid-Atlantic. Recipes from the past represent the use of seasonal whole foods that were cooked slowly. Some recipes became staples in the diets of the people of the Mid-Atlantic as recipes and cultural traditions were passed down through families for generations. However, over the centuries, technology changed the methods that people used to prepare foods and subsequently changed what people ate on a daily basis. With greater wealth came a wider variety of food options. Following the discovery of germs, technology improved preservation and canning techniques, which were followed by advancements in refrigeration and present-day flash freezing. Developments in transportation also drastically changed how food reached other parts of the region. On the homefront, improvements in insulation, the creation of smaller furnaces, the installation of indoor plumbing and air conditioning changed the way people cooked. Even the development of asphalt paving streets and snow tires increased urban sprawl and the development of supermarkets. Global trading also affected the development of food pathways as seasonal foods were now available at any given time at the local grocery story. Invasive species replacing native plants and animals also changed the abundance and availability in the food pathway hierarchy. In fact, all of these mitigating forces more than likely led to some foods literally falling out of favor because of a species becoming extinct, which can also be directly related to a decline in the appetite for certain foods. A prime example of such forces playing a role in changing the culinary landscape in the Mid-Atlantic is the decline of a forgotten delicacy: turtle soup, a food that was once eaten by the Indigenous peoples out of necessity and was highly favored by the wealthy from the seventeenth century until the early half of the twentieth century. In short, as technology changes, the types of foods that people eat will change eventually as well.

CHAPTER 1

The Indigenous Peoples of the Mid-Atlantic

If you know what people eat, you can find where they're from.
—*Frederick Opie*

Americal cuisine is as diverse as the history of the country. In every era, different dishes and food preparation methods are introduced and become part of the normal food routine. The food of the Mid-Atlantic encompasses the cultural identity of Native Americans, Africans and white European settlers and, later, immigrants from all over the world. Throughout the years from the beginning of the Americas to the present day, Mid-Atlantic cuisine has taken the influences from these groups and evolved around them. The cross-pollination of these groups is what makes Mid-Atlantic food what we think of today. Although each group had a different role in creating the food of the region, the foodways would be vastly different without the contribution of each group at a specific point in time.

Who were the Indigenous peoples of the Mid-Atlantic, and how did their existence and the development of their technology and subsequent culture influence the food pathways of the cuisine in the region? The Indigenous peoples of the Mid-Atlantic are believed to be descendants of the Paleo-Indians (also known as Paleoindians or Paleoamericans), who were the first people who entered, and subsequently inhabited, North and South America during the final climatic glacial events.

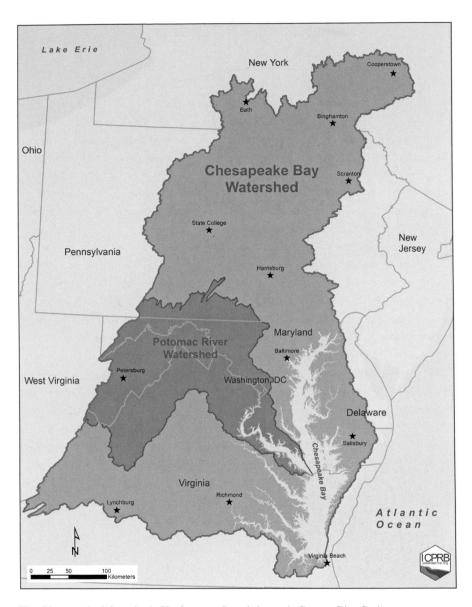

The Chesapeake Watershed. *The Interstate Commission on the Potomac River Basin.*

Ancient Human Migration

The specifics of Paleo-Indian migration to and throughout the Americas, including the exact dates and routes traveled, are subject to ongoing research and discussion. Most archaeologists hold the traditional theory that these early migrants were big-animal hunters who moved over a land-and-ice bridge known as Beringia between eastern Siberia and present-day western Alaska sometime between forty thousand and seventeen thousand years ago. Small, isolated groups of hunter-gatherers migrated alongside herds of large herbivores far into Alaska. Some archaeologists also have theorized that the origin of Paleo-Indians from central Asia, with widespread habitation of the Americas, may have occurred during the end of the last glacial period, around sixteen thousand to thirteen thousand years earlier. Ice-free corridors developed along the Pacific coast and valleys of North America, allowing animals, followed by humans, to migrate south into the interior of the continent. Archaeologists also believed that this group of Paleo-Indians migrated down the Pacific coast to South America, either on foot or by using primitive boats. Evidence of the latter would since have been covered by a sea level rise of hundreds of meters following the last ice age.

For the most part, archaeologists have identified three prehistoric periods in North America that were dominated by the presence of the Indigenous populations: the Paleo-Indian, the Archaic and the Woodland Periods.

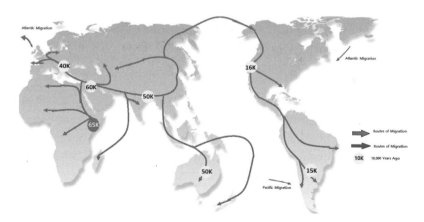

Ancient human migration. *Author's collection.*

The Paleo-Indian Period

In general, the human cultural life of the Mid-Atlantic region reaches back to 11000 BC. This period was marked by the use of the Clovis point, a prehistoric tool that was used for hunting. The Indigenous population along the Mid-Atlantic more than likely hunted white-tailed deer and turkey, caught fish, trapped small game mammals and subsisted on plant foraging. Food during this era would have been plentiful during the few warm months of the year. Groups moved from place to place as preferred resources were depleted and new supplies were sought. During much of the Early and Middle Paleo-Indian periods, inland bands are thought to have subsisted primarily through hunting now-extinct mammals such as the giant beaver, steppe wisent, musk ox, mastodon, woolly mammoth and ancient reindeer.

The Archaic Period

The second-most significant stage of Indigenous development occurred during the Archaic Period, which began about 10000 BC. The Archaic Period ushered in a very volatile time as the climate rapidly warmed. The tundra had transitioned into a shrubby, cold savannah, then an open forest and finally the mosaic of mixed deciduous and coniferous trees it is today. Sea levels rapidly rose due to the melting glaciers inundating some areas, whereas isostatic rebound exposed new lands and raised the elevations of other areas. By 7000 BC, the migratory patterns of fish and birds and most of the species of flora and fauna associated with the Mid-Atlantic today had become established in the region.

The human population also increased during the Archaic Period, due to the migrations of people from the southwest and because of the greater carrying capacity of the land due to numerous trees producing oily nuts, which were a major food source, and improved hunting technology. The Archaic Period peoples adopted the atlatl, which allowed hunters to throw spears from a greater distance and with greater force, and developed a more diverse set of stone points and carved hooks tailored to the species that were targeted. By the late part of the Archaic Period, most of the foods known to be gathered up until the period of English colonization were utilized at this time, particularly shellfish, as evidenced by the large shell middens that occupy numerous coastal sites throughout the Northeast and the Mid-Atlantic.

Ancient Indigenous tribe among the shell middens. *Getty Images.*

Even with the development of agriculture, which ushered in the Woodland Period around 1000 BC, the southern New England Algonquian peoples continued to rely on long-held hunting, fishing, collecting and foraging activities to supplement their diets. Food preparation was facilitated by the adoption of ceramic pottery around AD 500. The adoption of the bow and arrow around AD 700 greatly improved hunting prowess, as bow-and-arrow hunting was more stealthy than traditional spear and spear-throwing methods.

In areas such as the colder, rocky uplands and sandy shoals, where agriculture was greatly hampered, reliance on hunting and foraging assumed greater importance, but even in the most fertile areas, these activities were elemental to survival when food stores were thin at the end of the winter or when crops failed due to drought, pest or early frost.

It should also be noted that in the Mid-Atlantic, more Indigenous people were able to live in semi-sedentary camps. It is likely that as their tools, food storage capabilities and cooking vessels evolved, this type of subsistence allowed populations to remain at one camp for a longer period of time. During this era, it was observed that the adoption of sedentary farming began to develop.

THE WOODLAND PERIOD

The Archaic Period was followed by the Woodland Period, which in North American pre-Columbian cultures spanned a period from roughly 1000 BC until European contact in the eastern part of North America during the early part of the seventeenth century. During this time, Indigenous peoples continued to rely on long-held hunting, fishing, collecting and foraging activities to supplement their diets. Food preparation was facilitated with the adoption of ceramic pottery during the Middle Woodland Period around AD 500, which marked the beginning of the Point Peninsula Complex Indigenous culture. Point Peninsula ceramics were first introduced in Canada around 600 BC and then spread south into parts of North America. Point Peninsula pottery represented a new kind of technology in North America. Compared to existing stone vessels and ceramics that were thicker and less decorated, this new pottery has been characterized by "superior modeling of the clay with vessels being thinner, better fired and containing finer grit temper." The new pots were lighter in weight, easier to produce and heated faster than stone vessels. Where this new pottery technology originated is not known for sure.

In coastal regions, more Indigenous permanent settlements begin to form near iodized marshes that were rich in food resources. Since the dawn of time, humans tended to settle along rivers and lakes in both coastal and interior regions for maximum access to food resources. As a subsistence

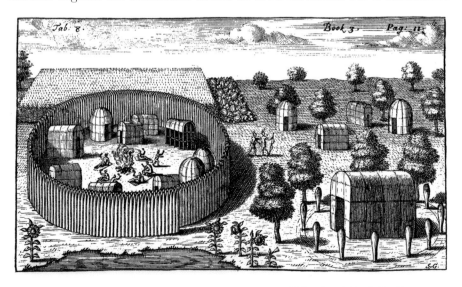

The Algonquin Farming Community engraving, 1705. *University of North Carolina at Chapel Hill.*

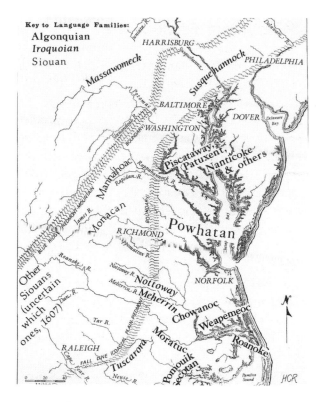

Chesapeake Bay region, 1607. By 1000, just before the English arrived, over fifty thousand people lived in the region. They are categorized into three linguistic groups: Algonquian, Iroquoian and Siouxan. *University of Oklahoma Press.*

strategy, Indigenous populations also took advantage of seasonally available resources, such as nuts, fish, shellfish and wild plants. Nuts were processed in large amounts, including hickory nuts and acorns. Many wild berries, including palm berries, blueberries, raspberries and strawberries, were eaten, as were wild grapes and persimmons. Shellfish formed an important part of the diet, attested to by numerous shell middens along the coast and interior rivers of the Chesapeake region. By the late Woodland Period (AD 500–1000), bow and arrow technology had gradually overtaken the use of the spear. In the areas surrounding the Chesapeake Bay and on the Eastern Shore of Maryland, the condensing of the bands of Indigenous populations was marked by the appearance of larger tribes, clans and confederacies that organized themselves into stratified political units known now as chiefdoms. They developed military and political alliances and practiced religious and spiritual ceremonies, as well as utilizing the crop rotation system that was aimed at giving thanks and keeping the world in balance. The primary Native groups that inhabited the Chesapeake Bay region and the many rivers included the Algonquin, Iroquois, Anacostank, Pamunkey, Powhatan, Mattapanient, Nangemeick and Tauxehent.

CHAPTER 2

Development of Agriculture

Agriculture developed in eastern North America independently with a series of domestication events, with the crops and methods of growing them spread by trade routes. The increasing use of horticulture led to the development of the Eastern Agricultural Complex, consisting of weedy seed plants, such as barley, and starchy, grain-like seeds of maygrass and knotweed, although the latter two crops were also eaten as leafy vegetables. To a lesser extent, Indigenous women also cultivated sunflowers for their oily seeds and Jerusalem artichokes for their fleshy, starchy tubers. Other crops included the *Cucurbita pepo*, an ancestor of various pumpkins, melons and squashes.

Around AD 500, the "three sisters"—maize, beans and squash—originally domesticated in Mesoamerica, were introduced to North America. By AD 1100, these crops had replaced the earlier crops of the Eastern Agricultural Complex, although they continued to be gathered in the wild. The three sisters became the cornerstone of a typical meal and were frequently consumed. Although historical evidence is scant, Native Americans did cultivate orchards of cherries and walnut trees. It is believed that lands cleared by fire were deliberately planted with various nut and fruit trees to provide food sources for future generations. The yields of the three sisters per acre was significantly higher but only after varieties adapted to the colder climate and shorter growing season. New varieties of *C. pepo* were introduced with edible flesh; these are now the familiar pumpkins, squashes and melons still grown throughout the United States. Although foods hunted and gathered from the wild, fish and shellfish supplemented the diet for coastal peoples, the three sisters heavily contributed to the bulk of the caloric intake for the Indigenous tribes.

The adoption of the three sisters was spread by migrations of Indigenous tribes that were originally from southern Ontario and western New York. This process was corroborated by the spread of the Point Peninsula Complex of pottery into New England from the west, as well as the intrusion of Algonquian genetic profiles into the population during the middle Woodland Period around 200 BC. The inhabitants of New England and the Mid-Atlantic during the Archaic Period shared genetic profiles that more closely associated with Catawba such as the Waccamaw but had absorbed the Algonquian tribes and adopted their language and culture. Later, Iroquoian peoples migrated into what is now New York and the Great Lakes, leading to an independent development of Eastern Algonquians. The culture and the ethnic divisions of the Woodland Period were more or less still in place by the time of European contact.

The amount of these crops being grown would not yet be sufficient as the main form of subsistence. Agricultural cultivation still greatly supplemented the gathering of wild plants. The adaptation of agriculture also meant that Indigenous groups became less mobile over time and people lived in permanently occupied villages. The Indigenous populations of the Chesapeake region continued to hunt and forage for aquatic animals, deer and turkey and also gathered plants and nuts from the forests.

For over a millennium, the Chesapeake Bay region has demonstrated a richly diverse Indigenous population that predates the appearance of Western European explorers who landed on the North American continent. Since about 3000 BC, the bounty of the Mid-Atlantic has sustained many Native bands, tribes and confederacies that organized themselves into stratified political units known now as chiefdoms, developed military and political alliances and practiced religious and spiritual ceremonies aimed at giving thanks and keeping the world in balance. They were all part of the massive Algonquian language group, with other tribes speaking Siouan or Iroquoian, that spanned the East Coast, up through the Great Lakes and Canada and even to the Great Plains and part of present-day California, all with distinct languages being related. The primary Native group that inhabited the Chesapeake Bay region and along the confluence of many rivers, including the Potomac and Anacostia, was and continues to be the Piscataway, along with several related groups, including the Algonquin, Iroquois, Anacostank, Pamunkey, Mattapanient, Nangemeick and Tauxehent.

Indigenous groups also exhibited early interaction with European explorers during the Late Woodland Period in the Chesapeake, but this would have been sporadic until 1607 with the appearance of John Smith and the English settlers. They officially ended the Late Woodland Period with the establishment of the English colony at Jamestown, Virginia. This was the beginning of the most significant alteration of the landscape and the natural processes that took place on a widespread scale. The establishment of Jamestown eventually upended Virginia Indian societies, including the once-powerful Powhatan Confederacy of Tsenacomoco. Many of the Algonquian-speaking tribes in the Tidewater region near Jamestown were led by Chief Powhatan (circa 1547–circa 1618), whose proper name was Wahunsenacawh (alternately spelled Wahunsenacah, Wahunsunacock or Wahunsonacock), at the time English settlers landed at Jamestown in 1607.

With few written records and relying on the oral history of Native tribes, it can only be presumed that the region around the Chesapeake Bay prior to the arrival of European settlers in the mid-1600s was filled primarily with mature, mixed deciduous forests; small areas of cleared land used mostly for sustainable agriculture; and slightly disturbed forests dotted around Native American settlements. Indigenous population densities were concentrated near river and bay shorelines and other water sources. There is evidence that Native Americans certainly used fire to clear settlement areas and garden plots and to manage habitat for game species, but such impacts were mostly confined to areas of only a few tens of acres.

The most significant alteration of the landscape and the natural processes that took place on a widespread scale following the arrival of European settlers in the region was the centuries of intensive land use. Beginning in 1642, when the first Africans were brought as slaves to St. Mary's City, Maryland, to grow and cultivate tobacco, the market was strong in Europe for this main commodity crop. Tobacco was labor-intensive in both cultivation and processing, and planters struggled to manage workers as farms became larger and more efficient. At first, indentured servants from England supplied much of the necessary labor, but as their economy improved at home in the Old World, fewer made passage to the colonies. Colonists in Virginia also turned to importing indentured and enslaved Africans to satisfy the labor demand in cultivating tobacco.

By the 1700s, the Native American population had been mostly eradicated by disease, famine and warfare, and the remnants of the tribes that remained were pushed farther westward by European colonization. All that remains from their centuries of habitation are campsite artifacts, still being unearthed; some notable bayside oyster middens; and anglicized names given to towns and rivers, such as Chesapeake, Patapsco, Potomac, Wicomico, Patuxent, Piscataway and Susquehanna. By the eighteenth and nineteenth centuries, anthropogenic activities had removed more than 90 percent of the original forest cover, leaving only a few patches of old-growth forest in remote, inaccessible mountain coves and ravines. With the decline of farming at the turn of the last century, much of the lowlands in the Mid-Atlantic region have returned to forest. Today, approximately 67 percent of the region is forested; 70 percent is in natural cover of one form or another.

Dining Habits and Eating Customs of Indigenous Peoples

For the most part, Indigenous peoples of North America were considered quite generous and hospitable, and guests to Indian homes were always welcomed with a refreshing drink of water and a share in whatever food was available or a meal when the food was completed and served. Groups of families would pool their resources, with men contributing meat and fish and women foraging, farming and preparing meals together. Because of the labor-intensive and time-consuming preparations, thick stews and breads constituted most meals.

Meals, however, were not structured in the way of the English colonists, who ideally ate three meals a day every day. The Native peoples, dependent on seasonal abundance, were said to eat plentiful foods during times of abundance (they were labeled "gluttons" by the English colonists), but during lean times, war, hunting expeditions or travels between seasonal encampments, Native peoples could go days without a proper meal, subsisting on dried slices of squash and a spoonful or two of parched cornmeal and whatever could be foraged along the way, having just enough food to stave off the hunger.

Women performed all the tasks of preparing and serving the food, with the chiefs, elders and guests being served first as a mark of respect and courtesy. Despite the marked division of labor, Native American tribes were based on a matrilineal culture, and there was more equitable treatment of women in Native American households than among the European settlers. It should be noted that women were not excluded from sitting to eat with men and were allowed to contribute to the mealtime conversation. In many tribes, the chiefs could also be women. In contrast, English colonial women were often excluded from the tables of formal dinners and ate separately with the children.

Foods were typically served when they were ready. Soups and various types of corn gruel were ladled into carved wooden or clay bowls and eaten with carved wooden spoons or spoons made from shells, whereas drier foods were placed in wooden or clay dishes, placed in baskets or simply set on mats of reeds. Meals could be eaten on mats of reeds on the ground in "Indian-style" seating or on benches built along the sides of the home. English colonial households ate in a similar fashion, as the utensils made of metals commonly used in England were expensive and difficult to import to the colonies.

THE REEMERGENCE OF INDIGENOUS FOODS

When food stores were low due to crop failures, drought, longer-than-usual winters and scarce game, the Native peoples resorted to other foods. It is known that the Native peoples would resort to eating bark, the youngest pine leaves and certain types of lichens in winter or when traveling long distances. In warmer seasons, the Native peoples could dig up worms and grubs, rely on catching smaller game and broaden their range. Since the European settlers did not understand how much foraging and gathering contributed to their diet, many Indians died of starvation or were forced into dangerous and menial work as their lands were usurped or forcibly sold by colonial and later state governments.

While Native American cuisine may seem to have all but disappeared, it is not as unfamiliar as many of us may think. Native American foodways are not one cuisine but several Indigenous pathways. Foods, procurement methods, cooking techniques, dining customs and religious observances varied greatly from tribe to tribe. Native Americans depended on the seasonal availability of local foods for sustenance. It should also be noted that some tribes placed great emphasis on structured villages and agriculture, whereas other tribes lived a more nomadic life, following their food source. When you really think about it, all of American cuisine is basically fusion cuisine. Cornbread, corn fritters, grits, succotash, Brunswick stew, chili and Boston baked beans—just to name a few—all grew out of Native American food traditions.

The major trend in Native American cookery in these modern times is to reach back to culinary roots in the pre-colonial past. This isn't easy because there are no accounts written by the Native Americans themselves of what they ate before the arrival of Europeans. There are a few descriptions of Indian dishes as they were recorded by explorers, colonists and settlers, and they make it possible to visualize Indigenous dishes through the "European gaze." For the most part, European newcomers had no clue what they were witnessing in terms of cultural customs of the Indigenous people they encountered, nor did they truly know what they were eating, as they attempted to describe what they saw and experienced based on their own personal and limited knowledge of Indigenous cultures. Unfortunately, pseudo-social cultural biases and subsequent translations and secondhand references often rendered inaccurate information. Since Indigenous cooking traditions were passed down orally and anchored in home territories, many were lost in the cultural upheavals that accompanied resettlement of tribes from their traditional homelands to government reservations. To re-create the culinary past, chefs today cite the need for historical research, a hands-on familiarity with local plants and a healthy dollop of imagination. It cannot be emphasized enough that the presence of Native Americans greatly contributed to the development of Indigenous food pathways, and for the most part, they laid the foundation for what is considered Mid-Atlantic cuisine and also helped to define the modern cuisine of America.

BRUNSWICK STEW

Once again, trying to unravel the culinary origins and foodways of early American cuisine in the Mid-Atlantic literally becomes a chase down a rabbit hole. Such is the case of Brunswick stew. The original Brunswick stew was a squirrel soup with onions and can be traced to Neolithic times, when hunter-gatherers put whatever game they could find in the pot with whatever vegetables were in season. Brunswick stew was originally made by several of the Native American tribes long before European colonists arrived in the New World. For centuries, squirrels were a popular and important source of food for the Mid-Atlantic region.

The best-documented early evidence of this stew is from Brunswick County, Virginia. In 1828, Dr. Creed Haskins, a member of the Virginia House of Delegates from 1839 to 1841, took a group of friends on a hunting expedition on the banks of the Nottaway River. While they were off hunting, his enslaved camp cook, known as Uncle Jimmy Matthews, resourcefully trapped some squirrels and used them in preparation of a thick soup with onions and stale bread. Upon their return, the cold and starving hunters were hesitant to try the stew made with squirrel meat, but their hunger won out. They liked the thick, warm stew so much that they asked for another helping. This concoction became known as the first Brunswick stew. It is rumored that Jimmy Matthews was asked by Haskins to re-create his stew cooked in a large pot for a political rally for President Andrew Jackson. Without fail, Brunswick stew soon became one of the principal attractions of political rallies conducted by the Whigs and Democrats, and it was served at cockfights, family reunions, tobacco curings and other Virginia gatherings.

The original Brunswick stew was made primarily with squirrel and few vegetables. This version of the recipe is made with chicken thighs and barbecued beef brisket, which adds another dimension of flavor.

Serves 8 to 12

1 tablespoon vegetable oil
2 large onions, chopped
3 garlic cloves, minced
4 cups beef stock
2 pounds chicken thighs
1 28-ounce can crushed tomatoes, with the juices

1 15-ounce can white shoepeg corn, drained (use fresh if in season)
1 15-ounce can baby lima beans, drained (use fresh if in season)
1 15-ounce can creamed corn
1 tablespoon brown sugar
1 tablespoon Worcestershire sauce
⅛ teaspoon cayenne pepper
Kosher salt, to taste
Freshly ground black pepper, to taste
1 ½ pounds Yukon Gold potatoes, peeled, diced into 2-inch cubes
1 pound shredded barbecued beef brisket (see page 166)
½ tablespoon fresh lemon juice
Crusty bread, for serving

Heat the oil in a 5-quart Dutch oven or a large pot over medium-high heat until the oil is shimmering. Sauté onions and garlic in the hot oil for 3 to 5 minutes or until tender.

Add the beef stock, chicken thighs, tomatoes, whole kernel corn, lima beans, creamed corn, brown sugar, Worcestershire sauce, cayenne pepper, salt and black pepper to taste. Bring the Dutch oven to a boil. Cover and reduce heat to a simmer and cook, stirring occasionally, for 2 hours.

Uncover the Dutch oven. Using two forks, shred the chicken into large pieces and remove the bones. Add the potatoes and cook for 20 to 25 minutes or until potatoes are fork tender.

Add the brisket and lemon juice. Continue to allow the stew to simmer uncovered for 35 minutes or longer, until the stew slightly thickens.

To serve, ladle the stew into soup bowls and serve with a hearty, rustic crusty bread if desired.

VENISON AND GREEN CORN STEW

Venison (deer) has been a staple for Indigenous people for thousands of years. Long before the Columbian Exchange and the arrival of chicken, beef, pork or even lamb to North America, wild game like venison, rabbit, moose and elk was hunted by Indigenous tribes. Venison was also eaten by Europeans prior to the colonization of the Americas. Historically, venison was considered a symbol of status and wealth.

This recipe for venison and green corn stew is based on a Native American recipe from the Caughnawaga of the Iroquois Confederacy, who traveled throughout the Mid-Atlantic, from Upstate New York to Pennsylvania and across the Ohio River Valley. The recipe comes from an eyewitness account by Colonel James Smith (1737–1813), who was a frontiersman, farmer and soldier in British North America. Smith was captured by the Delaware (Lanape) tribe in 1755 and eventually adopted by the Caughnawaga. Upon his adoption into the tribe, a feast was held in his honor where he described a stew made of venison and green corn. Smith published his memoirs in 1799, titled An Account of the Remarkable Occurrences in the Life and Travels of Col. James Smith During His Captivity with the Indians in the Years 1755–1759, *in which this passage appears:*

"After this ceremony was over, I was introduced to my new kin, and told that I was to attend a feast that evening, which I did. And as the custom was, they gave me also a bowl and wooden spoon, which I carried with me to the place, where there was a number of large brass kettles full of boiled venison and green corn; every one advanced with his bowl and spoon, and had his share given him. After this, one of the chiefs made a short speech, and then we began to eat."

Smith spent five years with the tribe before returning to "civilization." In 1765, he led the "Black Boys," a group of Pennsylvania men, in a nine-month rebellion against British rule ten years before the outbreak of the American Revolutionary War. He participated in the war as a colonel of the Pennsylvania militia and was later elected a legislator in the Kentucky General Assembly. Smith became a Presbyterian missionary to the Native Americans, aided by the knowledge he had acquired of their customs in his early captivity.

VENISON AND GREEN CORN STEW

Serves 6

1 cup dried corn kernels
½ cup chopped beef suet
3 pounds venison stew meat (shoulder, neck, shank, rump)
2 pounds deer (or beef soup) bones
3 large onions, chopped
3 cloves garlic, minced
Salt, to taste
Ground white pepper, to taste
4 cups beef stock, or as needed
Fresh chopped parsley, for garnish

Cover corn with 2 cups of water. Bring to a boil, boil 1 minute and remove from heat. Cover pot and let sit for an hour.

Cut meat into 1-inch cubes. Heat the suet in a heavy cast-iron pot. Sear the meat along with the bones, and when they are browned, remove and put aside. Sauté onions and garlic in the same pot until onions are translucent. Add the salt and pepper to taste.

Return the meat and bones to the stew pot. Add the corn with its liquid. Add beef stock to cover. Bring mixture slowly to a simmer and simmer gently until meat and corn are both tender, 1½ to 2 hours. Remove bones. Taste and adjust the seasoning with salt and pepper, if needed.

Ladle the soup into serving bowls and garnish with parsley. Serve immediately.

Cook's Notes:
For those not familiar with suet, it is the fat of either beef or mutton, usually taken from around the kidneys and loins. It has a whitish, crumbly appearance. In supermarkets, it may be shredded or grated and mixed with a small amount of flour. You may use vegetable shortening like Crisco as a substitute, which has a similar melting point to suet. The flavor and texture will not be quite the same, but it will be closer than using butter alone. You can also substitute equal parts by volume of rendered fat (beef, pork or chicken) that has been allowed to solidify. Any of these will result in a slightly moister product than if made with

suet but should be acceptable. If you have access to a health food store or other store catering to vegetarians, you may be able to find a vegetarian suet alternative.

If venison is not readily available, feel free to use beef, lamb or bison as suitable substitutes.

Dried corn is available wherever there are Spanish markets, but if you must substitute, whole hominy works better than fresh or frozen corn kernels, which will toughen with long cooking.

FRIED LOBSTER TAILS WITH SKUNK BEAN SUCCOTASH

The skunk bean is a rare bean that the Haudenosaunee (Iroquois) people have been growing for many generations. Also known as the Chester skunk bean, the heirloom variety has been cultivated in Chester, Vermont, for many years. Very productive and adapted to short season climates, skunk beans are shaped like lima beans but have distinguishing black and white streaks. Some beans also have reverse markings, with the occasional all-black appearing in the crop. As a dry bean, this variety will cook quickly and can be used in a number of dishes, including soup and stews.

Serves 6

For the skunk beans:
2 cups chicken broth or water
Pinch of salt
2 pounds dried skunk beans
2 tablespoons butter

For the succotash:
2 tablespoons vegetable oil
1 ½ cups chopped onion
Kosher salt, to taste
1 large garlic clove, minced
3 cups chopped fresh tomatoes
2 ¼ cups fresh yellow corn kernels
2 cups cooked skunk beans
Freshly ground black pepper, to taste
2 tablespoons chopped fresh parsley

For the lobster tails:
6 fresh, uncooked lobster tails
Vegetable oil, for frying
1 cup self-rising flour
2 ½ teaspoons kosher salt
1 teaspoon ground black pepper
¼ teaspoon Old Bay Seasoning
2 large eggs, lightly beaten

Fried lobster and skunk bean succotash. *Author's collection.*

For the skunk beans:

Add 2 cups of chicken broth or water and the salt to a medium saucepan. Add the beans. Cover and bring to a boil over medium heat. Uncover, reduce heat and simmer until beans are tender and creamy, about 30 minutes. Using a colander, drain the liquid and add the butter and set aside.

For the succotash:

Heat oil in a large cast-iron skillet over medium heat. Add onion and sprinkle with salt to taste. Sauté onion until soft and translucent, about 5 minutes. Add garlic; stir until fragrant, about 1 minute. Add tomatoes and corn. Reduce heat to medium-low, cover and simmer until corn is tender and tomatoes are soft, about 30 minutes, stirring occasionally. Stir in the skunk beans and season to taste with salt and pepper. Stir in parsley.

For the lobster tails:

Remove shell completely around lobster tail meat, leaving fins on. Pour the oil to a depth of 1½ inches in a small Dutch oven; heat oil over medium to 325 degrees Fahrenheit. Stir together flour, salt, pepper and Old Bay Seasoning in a medium bowl. Dip lobster tails in beaten eggs; dredge in flour mixture, shaking off any excess. Cook in hot oil until golden brown and crispy, 2 to 2½ minutes per side. Remove the tails from the oil and drain on paper towels.

To serve, spoon the succotash onto a plate and arrange the fried lobster tails on top of the vegetables.

Cook's Notes:

If skunk beans are unavailable, 2 cups of fresh lima beans (from about 2 pounds pods) or 10 to 11 ounces of frozen baby lima beans, thawed, can be used as a substitute in this dish.

SAUTÉED RAMPS

The plant known scientifically as Allium tricoccum is also known as the wild leek, the wild onion or spring tonic, but it is most commonly called the ramp. The ramp finds its native home in the moist, shady mountainous forests of eastern North America. However, its range stretches from Nova Scotia down through to North Carolina and Georgia and west to Missouri and Iowa. Despite this range, the ramp is commonly referred to as an Appalachian vegetable due to the mountain region's favorable growing conditions, as well as the plant's centrality in the region's diet, particularly in the hill country of West Virginia, where ramps typically grow under the shade of deciduous trees in rich, loamy soil.

These slow-growing plants can often be found in large colonies and are distinguished by their two slender, glossy green leaves that grow from bulbs. The leaves wither by the time the stalk matures, on which clusters of small white flowers grow. As the plant matures, the layered bulbs also grow larger. With a small white bulb and hairy root, they resemble scallions and are foraged from shady, woody areas during just a few weeks from late April to early June.

Being one of the first greens to appear in the spring, ramps were once considered an important food source by Indigenous tribes throughout North America in providing vitamins and minerals that had not been available during the winter. It is similar in taste to a spring onion, but with an offensively aromatic pungency that is closer to garlic. The ramp's bulb and its leaves are consumed when the plant is still young. And because of their high vitamin content and blood-cleansing properties, ramps were highly prized by Indigenous peoples for their nutritional value and medicinal purposes. The Cherokee boiled or fried the young plants, while the Iroquois consumed them seasoned with salt and pepper. Both the Ojibwa and Menominee dried and stored parts of the ramp to be saved for winter months. European colonists also consumed ramps—because they offered variation in a relatively limited diet—by frying them in butter or animal fat or eating them raw.

The Chippewa decocted the root to induce vomiting, while the Cherokee consumed the ramp to treat coughs and colds and also made it into a poultice that was applied to bee stings. The Cherokee also made a juice from the plant to treat earaches. A tonic of the plant was used by the Iroquois to treat intestinal worms.

SAUTÉED RAMPS

Mountain folk who lived in West Virginia and North Carolina were commonly referred to as "ramp-eaters," and they have enjoyed gathering at ramp festivals since the 1930s.

Today, ramps appear for a fleeting moment at farmers' markets and in specialty grocery stores in early spring. Most home cooks commonly prepare ramps fried with potatoes in bacon fat or scrambled with eggs and served with bacon, pinto beans and cornbread. Ramps can also be pickled or used in soups and other foods in place of onions and garlic.

Serves 2 to 3

2 bunches young ramps
1 tablespoon olive oil
Salt, to taste
Freshly ground black pepper, to taste

Fill a large bowl with cold water, then place one bunch of ramps in the water. Swish them around to remove as much soil debris as possible, then remove them from the bowl and give them a second rinse under running water to remove any remaining grit. Change the water and do the same with the second bunch of ramps. Place the ramps on a dry paper towel, then top with another paper towel and pat out as much water as possible.

With a sharp chef's knife, chop off any of the remaining hairy roots. Set aside.

In a large cast-iron skillet, heat the olive oil over medium-high heat. Swirl around to coat the pan. Add the ramps to the skillet and cook, turning occasionally, until the ramp leaves are slightly wilted and the white parts are translucent and lightly golden in color. Season lightly with salt and a dash of black pepper.

Serve immediately.

ROASTED TURKEY

America owes its tradition of the Thanksgiving feast to a man named Tisquantum (circa 1585–1622), more commonly known as Squanto. He was a member of the Patuxet tribe and is best known for being an early liaison between the Native populations in southern New England and the Mayflower Pilgrims. As a child, Squanto was kidnapped by an English sea captain named Thomas Hunt and sold into slavery in the city of Málaga, Spain. Squanto was among a number of captives bought by local monks who focused on their education and evangelization, and as a result, he learned to speak Spanish, French and English. Squanto eventually traveled to England and from there returned to North America in 1619, only to find that his village and tribe had been wiped out by an epidemic infection, making Squanto the last of the Patuxet.

When the Mayflower landed in 1620, Squanto was one of the first Native Americans the members of the Plymouth colony encountered. As a diplomat, he worked to broker peaceable relations between the Pilgrims and the Wampanoag. He played a key role in the early meetings in March 1621, partly because he spoke English. He then lived with the Pilgrims for two years, acting as a translator, guide and advisor. During this time, he also saved the colony from starvation by teaching the settlers how to sow, plant and fertilize native crops—including corn and squash, which proved vital since the seeds that the Pilgrims had brought from England largely failed. He also taught the settlers how to fish and to tap maple trees for their sweet sap.

Because of Squanto's central role in the survival of the Plymouth colony, a feast was held to commemorate the event. It was referred to at the time as the "Harvest Celebration of 1621" and is considered the first Thanksgiving that took place in the colony. From historical journals, the menu at the first Thanksgiving celebration between the Pilgrims and the Wampanoag consisted of wild game that included venison, goose, duck, pigeon and turkey; and seafood such as mussels, clams, oysters, lobsters, bass and eels. A combination of wild and cultivated crops including chestnuts, walnuts, squash, beans and dishes made from dried corn was also served.

ROASTED TURKEY

Serves 10 to 12

For the brine:
1 12- to 14-pound turkey
2½ cups kosher salt, plus more if needed
1 cup white sugar
3 bay leaves
1 tablespoon black peppercorns, cracked, more as needed
3 sprigs each fresh rosemary, thyme, sage and marjoram

For the turkey:
Salt, to taste
Freshly ground black pepper, to taste
1 large yellow onion, peeled and quartered
2 ribs of celery, roughly chopped
2 carrots, peeled and roughly chopped
½ lemon
1 stick of unsalted butter, sliced for basting

For the gravy:
1 cup defatted pan juices from the roasted turkey
1 cup chicken stock

Remove the turkey from the packaging and rinse under cold water.

Place the turkey on a rack in its roasting pan and prepare the brine. Combine the salt, sugar, bay leaves, pepper, rosemary, thyme, sage and marjoram with 2½ gallons of water in a large 4- to 6-gallon container or cooler large enough to hold the turkey comfortably. Stir until salt and sugar dissolve. Place the turkey in brining solution and refrigerate or ice overnight.

The following day, prepare to cook the turkey.

Preheat oven to 425 degrees Fahrenheit.

Remove the turkey from the brining solution; drain well and pat very dry with clean paper towels. Discard brine. Set the turkey, breast side up, on a roasting rack set into a large roasting pan. Season with salt and pepper, then fill the cavity with onion, celery, carrots and lemon. Fold wings under the bird. Truss the turkey up by the legs using kitchen twine. Roast the turkey for 35 minutes, basting with butter every 10 minutes.

Reduce the oven temperature to 350 degrees Fahrenheit and roast approximately 3 hours more, basting bird every 30 minutes with drippings and butter. If the breast of the turkey is browning too quickly, tent the bird with aluminum foil and continue to cook until an instant-read thermometer inserted into the thickest part of the thigh without touching bone registers 165 degrees Fahrenheit.

Remove the turkey from the oven and allow to rest for 30 minutes.

Meanwhile, make a gravy from the pan drippings. Discarding any solid vegetables used in roasting the main meat dish, pour the pan juices into a glass measuring cup and let stand for 10 minutes. Skim off any fat that forms on the surface. Heat a cast-iron skillet over high heat and pour in the fat/grease-free pan juices, then the chicken stock. Bring to a boil, stirring with a wooden spoon until smooth. Pour into a gravy boat.

To serve, transfer the turkey to a serving platter and carve into the desired pieces. Serve with the pan gravy on the side.

CORNBREAD

Native Americans have been using ground corn (maize) as food for thousands of years, long before Europeans arrived in the New World. European settlers learned the original recipes and processes for corn dishes from Indigenous tribes engaged in agricultural practices, and soon they devised recipes using cornmeal in breads similar to those made with grains available in Europe. Cornbread was popular during the American Civil War because it was inexpensive and could be made in many different forms, from high-rising, fluffy loaves and muffins to simply fried and unleavened to make pone, corn fritters and hoecakes. Cornbread has its foundations in Native American foodways, and subsequently, it has become one of the cornerstones of the cuisine of the southern United States.

Makes one 9-inch round of bread

2 tablespoons vegetable oil
1 cup yellow cornmeal
1 cup all-purpose flour
2½ teaspoons baking powder
½ teaspoon baking soda
2 tablespoons sugar
1 teaspoon salt
2 eggs, beaten
1 cup buttermilk
½ stick butter

Preheat the oven to 425 degrees Fahrenheit.

Add the vegetable oil to a 9-inch cast-iron skillet and swirl to coat the skillet. Place the skillet in the oven to heat the oil.

Combine the cornmeal, flour, baking powder, baking soda, sugar and salt in a large bowl. In a smaller bowl, combine the eggs and buttermilk. Combine the liquid and dry ingredients.

Add the butter to the skillet and place in the oven until the butter is sizzling. Pour the butter into the batter and stir well.

Place the skillet filled with cornbread batter in the oven and cook until a wooden toothpick inserted in the center comes out clean, about 25 minutes.

Cut into wedges and serve hot.

PAWPAW PUDDING

For centuries, the North American pawpaw has been a delicious food source for Native Americans, European explorers, settlers and wild animals. Pawpaws were well known to several founding fathers, including George Washington, who was fond of pawpaw fruit and ate them for dessert when they were in season. Thomas Jefferson cultivated pawpaw trees on his vast plantation, Monticello. It's hard to overstate the importance of pawpaws to the early pioneers. As the first settlers left the established colonies and pushed westward, they often subsisted on wild game and the highly nutritious pawpaws that grew abundantly. The Lewis and Clark Expedition from May 1804 to September 1806, also known as the Corps of Discovery Expedition, was the first American expedition to cross the western portion of the United States. President Thomas Jefferson commissioned the expedition shortly after the Louisiana Purchase in 1803 to explore and map the newly acquired territory, to find a practical route across the western half of the continent and to establish an American presence in this territory before Britain and other European powers tried to claim

Pawpaw pudding with whipped cream. *Author's collection.*

it. The campaign's secondary objectives were scientific and economic: to study the area's plants, animal life and geography and to establish trade with local Native American tribes. Tasked with keeping a written record of their journey, Lewis and Clark as well as several other members of the expedition kept daily journals of their activities. Sergeants John Ordway and Patrick Gass, as well as Private Robert Frazer, were among those who also kept records of the journey. According to the first published account of the expedition by Gass, which appeared in 1810, during the fall of 1806, explorers Lewis and Clark, a slave known only as York (owned by Clark) and their guide (a Native American woman named Sacajawea) depended almost entirely on wild pawpaws and nuts when their rations ran low and game was scarce. This was documented in a journal entry dated September 18, 1806, which notes that the men were "entirely out of provisions" but "appear perfectly contented and tell us that they can live very well on the pappaws."

As the United States became more industrialized, the popularity of the fruit declined, and it fell into obscurity as it was replaced by more familiar cultivated fruits, such as apples, pears and cherries. Pawpaw is so delicate that it does not travel well. The fruit has a limited shelf life, being in season only during early to mid-September, making it difficult to stock in commercial grocery stores. However, pawpaws can be found at local farmers' markets along the East Coast and in the Mid-Atlantic when they are in season.

The pawpaw is a strange fruit that tastes like a hybrid of sweet potatoes, bananas, papayas, avocados and really ripe mangoes. This odd, goopy-textured, tropical-like fruit whose name rhymes with "heehaw" can be found scattered all over the country, but recipes abound largely in West Virginia and nearby states like Kentucky, Ohio and Indiana. Pawpaw pudding is usually served as a holiday dessert during Thanksgiving and Christmas.

Statue of York, Louisville, Kentucky. The eight-foot-tall sculpture created by Ed Hamilton was commissioned and erected by the City of Louisville in commemoration of the 200th anniversary of Lewis and Clark's historical trip. York (circa 1770–circa 1830) was an enslaved man owned by William Clark and later became a significant member of the Corps of Discovery Expedition from 1803 through 1806. William Clark inherited York as property when the elder Clark died, and the two were around the same age. More than likely, York was a childhood companion to Clark. York is often mentioned in the journals kept by both Lewis and Clark throughout the course of the expedition. The journals indicate that York was allowed to hunt, which was notable because African Americans, free or enslaved, were not allowed to own or handle guns. These journal entries indicate that he experienced freedoms that few enslaved people had, though these freedoms would be revoked upon his return to the Clark plantation. When the Corps of Discovery returned from the expedition, each member—except York—received double pay and 320 acres of land. York, on the other hand, returned to slavery. York was finally freed sometime after 1815. The York statue sits atop the Belvedere, located at the corner of Fifth and Main Streets, overlooking the Ohio River. *Author's collection.*

PAWPAW PUDDING

Serves 12

½ cup butter, melted, plus more for the baking dish
2 cups granulated white sugar
1 ½ cups all-purpose flour
1 teaspoon baking powder
¼ teaspoon salt
½ teaspoon ground cinnamon
¼ teaspoon ground ginger
¼ teaspoon ground nutmeg
3 large eggs
2 cups pawpaw pulp, thawed if frozen
1 ½ cups whole milk
1 teaspoon pure vanilla extract
Lightly sweetened whipped cream, for serving

Preheat oven to 350 degrees Fahrenheit. Grease a 13x9x2-inch baking dish.

In a large mixing bowl, whisk together sugar, flour, baking powder, salt, cinnamon, ginger and nutmeg.

In another large bowl, whisk together eggs and pawpaw pulp until smooth. Whisk in milk and vanilla. Whisk in melted butter. Pour into sugar mixture and stir only until combined.

Pour batter into prepared dish. Bake for 50 minutes or until just set in the center. Cool to room temperature on a wire rack before cutting.

Serve with a dollop of sweetened whipped cream.

. . . .

50

CHAPTER 3

Where the African Diaspora Meets the Colonial Crossroads

THE COLUMBIAN EXCHANGE

The food that was eaten at this time was simply what Natives foraged, hunted and grew and what the Europeans brought over that would grow on the Atlantic Coastal Plain. Mid-Atlantic cuisine was not what we conceptualize as it exists today until the Columbian Exchange occurred.

The Columbian Exchange refers to the exchange of ideas, food crops, populations and diseases between the New World and the Old World following the second voyage to the Americas by Christopher Columbus in 1493. The Old World, which included Europe and the entire Eastern Hemisphere, benefited from the Columbian Exchange in a number of ways. The discoveries of new supplies of natural resources, like metals such as gold and silver, are perhaps the best known. But the Old World also gained new staple crops, such as potatoes, sweet potatoes, maize and cassava. Less calorie-intensive foods, such as tomatoes, chili peppers, cacao, peanuts and pineapples, were also introduced and are now culinary centerpieces in many Old World countries, namely Italy, Greece and other Mediterranean countries (tomatoes), India and Korea (chili peppers), Hungary (paprika, made from chili peppers) and Malaysia and Thailand (chili peppers and pineapples).

The Columbian Exchange changed American foodways in a large sense. This exchange of food, livestock, diseases and humans as commodities created a massive cultural shift in the Americas. Moreover, the changes

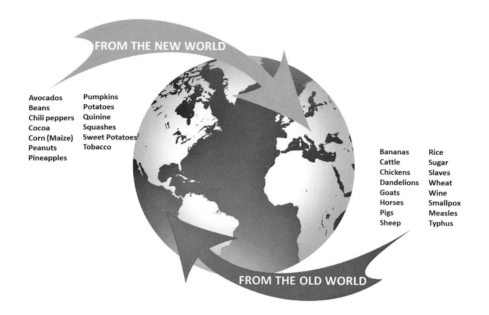

The Columbian Exchange. *Author's collection.*

in agriculture significantly altered and changed global populations. The cultivation of financially lucrative crops like tobacco and sugar in the Americas, along with the devastation of Indigenous populations that were enslaved and died from disease, resulted in a demand for labor. That demand on labor was met by the Columbian Exchange, which gave rise to the transatlantic slave trade, also known as the Middle Passage, which was the largest abduction, deportation, forced movement and enslavement of human beings in the collective memory of human history and a determining factor in the world economy between the fifteenth and eighteenth centuries.

AFRICAN ROOTS: FROM THE MIDDLE PASSAGE TO SLAVERY

Another example of how the Columbian Exchange altered food pathways and food identity can be found in colonial America beginning with the transatlantic slave trade. Food was both a form of resistance for and a tool of control over enslaved people. Over the course of four hundred years, millions of enslaved Africans were forcibly transported to the Americas and the Caribbean across the Atlantic Ocean. This forced migration is known as the Middle Passage. Slavers used a rigorous system of violence to turn human beings into "commodities" during the Middle Passage, and food was an important element of this process. Rations were scientifically calculated to provide the cheapest, minimal nutrition to keep the enslaved people alive.

Most often, African staple foods such as okra, rice and kidney and lima beans were transported on slave ships along with the human cargo. For the most part, these crops were selected because they remain palatable long after harvesting and were thus ideal for use on the slow voyage from Africa. The food was to ensure that the slaves were able to eat while traveling in fetid conditions to their new way of life in perpetual servitude. There were many other crops that traveled as well, such as watermelon, yams, guinea melon, millet and sesame. It should also be noted that all the edible parts of these nonnative plants flourished once they had been planted in the colonies. Because these crops were able to blend and form new food pathways, many of them can still be found in dishes cooked in kitchens across America.

ON BOARD A SLAVE-SHIP.

The shackling of enslaved Africans on board a slave ship, circa 1830. Heroes of Britain, *1890*.

Think about it—without these plants being brought over, some of the staple Mid-Atlantic foods that we enjoy today would not be in existence.

Mid-Atlantic dishes can be perceived as the quintessential American cuisine, and it has been established that it derived from a complex blend of Native American, European and African origins. While Mid-Atlantic food has evolved from sources and cultures of diverse regions, classes, races and ethnicities, African and African American slaves have one of the strongest yet least recognized food pathways. For enslaved people, cooking was about culture and community as much as it was about survival. Through the horrors of the Middle Passage and bondage in North America, generations of slaves preserved and created culinary traditions that remain strong today.

Unwittingly, in forging a new cultural food identity, slave owners often had enslaved African women be their cooks. These dishes focused mainly on European-style cooking, borrowing heavily from the English and French culinary traditions. In the beginning, many slave owners, like the early Spaniards in Latin American colonies, refused to eat the native food brought from Africa. Dietary prejudices being among our most unreasonable biases, such culinary strangers could be tolerated in the cabin of the enslaved, but they were not at first considered suitable for the slave owner's table.

In addition to their meager rations, enslaved Africans were also given the discarded foods from their masters' tables that did not satisfy their hunger. From growing basic crops for their own use, utilizing leftovers and gathering locally available ingredients like kale, dandelion tops, collards and mustard greens, resourceful enslaved African cooks learned to improvise in their own kitchens. Because slave owners "lived high on the hog" by taking the best cuts of meat for their own consumption, slaves made use of the offal and other discarded animal parts and developed recipes that included tripe, oxtails, intestines, pigs' ears, feet and jowls, among others. They also used lots of onions, peppers, garlic and herbs to add flavor to their dishes.

As more and more ingredients became available from the European traders, dishes evolved to become part of the typical slave household's meals. Many of the enslaved also fished and hunted for wild game to supplement their diets. Eating opossums, squirrels, rabbits, turtles and raccoons was not uncommon for the era.

Enslaved African cooks assigned to the main house introduced their native African crops and foods to their masters. Integrating their culinary skills into the service of the main house, enslaved African cooks introduced deep-fat frying, a cooking technique that originated in Africa. The African slave

VOL. XII.—No. 68.—M

THE COOK.

Female cook in her kitchen, Virginia, early 1850s. Harper's New Monthly Magazine, *1856*.

cooks also brought other techniques, such as toasting in the ashes, steaming in leaves and one-pot stewing.

Eventually, the slave diet found its way to the master's table. This style of cooking is still common among African Americans today, especially in the South. In the Mid-Atlantic, dishes emerged like stuffed ham, where slaves used the traditional African cooking method of packing the jowls of a hog with greens and spices and slowly simmering it to create this uniquely Maryland delicacy.

Enslaved Africans passed down their techniques, such as preparing and seasoning foods, to their children, who in turn passed it down to their children. While acknowledging that African American cooking is certainly a derivative of African cuisine, it largely developed as a result of the exigencies of life as a slave. The evolution of the slave cook being elevated to the level of a chef can be seen in the paths of Hercules Posey (circa 1748–1812) and James Hemings (1765–1801). As a result, African slave cooks were becoming the intermediary links in the melding of African and European culinary cultures, and so colonial plantation families began enjoying creations of "African" vegetables, seeds and starches. After the slave owners and their wives readily accepted the African versions of European dishes, they began to take ownership of some of the dishes inspired by their enslaved cooks. Without the slave owner's acceptance, many American dishes would lack any African influence.

Enslaved Africans developed a uniquely African American culture, presence and influence in the Mid-Atlantic from over four hundred years of exchange, innovation and resilience, which has been strongly preserved by today's African American cuisine. Many of the foods that we enjoy today have their roots in enslaved people's blood, sweat, tears, toil, tradition and creativity. It also includes the food that slaves incorporated into their diets after emancipation. Slave foods eventually transitioned into a food pathway that became a source of pride in the African American community. The tastes and traditions of the African cooking ways have been embraced and evolved into the "soul food" we know today.

Food Is Power

Colonization in the Americas was a violent process that fundamentally altered the ways of life of the colonized and the enslaved. Food has always been a fundamental tool in the process of colonization. Through food, social and cultural norms are conveyed and also violated. As a result of the Columbian Exchange, the Indigenous people of the Americas encountered a radically different food system with the arrival of the Europeans, and the enslaved Africans had to adapt and assimilate food as a matter of survival. The legacy of this system is very present in the food practices of modern society. Yet, we must never forget that the practice of colonization has always been a contested matter as groups have negotiated spaces within this process. Indigenous foods and African foods remain as present in contemporary American diets as do European foods. Understanding the history of food and eating practices in different contexts can help us understand that the practice of eating is inherently complex. Food choices are influenced and constrained by cultural values and are an important part of the construction and maintenance of social identity. In that sense, food has never merely been about the simple act of pleasurable consumption—food is history that is culturally transmitted, and it is identity. And therefore, food is power.

CHAPTER 4

The Evolution of Fusion Cooking in Colonial America

THE WYE PLANTATION AND THE LLOYD FAMILY COOKBOOKS

Handwritten cookbooks and household manuals from slave plantations are surprisingly well preserved and give us a glimpse of the domestic life of prominent slave-owning families in America. By using the cookbooks, we can better understand the roles of women, both white and Black, in running a plantation. Documented evidence of such cookbooks and household manuals can be found at the Wye Plantation, where the estate and its surrounding grounds hold a unique place in American history.

The Wye Plantation, located in Talbot County, Maryland, was settled in the 1650s by a Welsh Puritan and wealthy planter, Edward Lloyd. Between 1781 and 1784, the main house was built by his great-great-grandson Edward Lloyd IV. Near the house is an orangery, a rare survivor of an early garden greenhouse structure where orange and lemon trees were cultivated; it still contains its original eighteenth-century heating system of hot air ducts. The Wye Plantation was designated a National Historic Landmark in 1970.

At one time, the plantation surrounding the house encompassed 42,000 acres and housed over one thousand slaves. Though the land has shrunk to roughly 1,300 acres today, it is still owned by the descendants of Edward Lloyd, now in their eleventh generation on the property. Frederick Douglass (circa 1818–1895), a former slave who rose to prominence as a social reformer, abolitionist, orator, writer and statesman, lived on the plantation around the ages of seven and eight and later wrote extensively of the brutal conditions

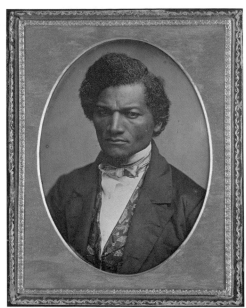

Left: Edward Lloyd IV (1744–1796). *New York City Public Library*.

Right: Frederick Douglass (1818–1895). *Library of Congress*.

of the plantation in his autobiography, *Narrative of the Life of Frederick Douglass, an American Slave* (1845).

Most of the recipes found in the Lloyd family cookbooks were on a small scale. It can be assumed that most of the cooking was conducted by African American women, enslaved and later free. Food historian Katherine Harbury noted that these plantation family cookbooks were also created by upper-class women to showcase the duty of the housewife to spread her knowledge to her daughters and educate them in the art of cooking and presentation. This is evident in the Lloyd family cookbooks, where recipes are scattered throughout each volume. Some of the recipes were written in a childish script, indicating that the cookbooks were probably used to teach the girls to read, write and cook at the same time. In 1851, Edward Lloyd VII (1825–1907) married Mary Key (1825–1923), the daughter of Charles Howard, Esq., of Baltimore. Three of their children appear in the cookbooks: Alicia Lloyd Oliver (1855–1942), son McBlair Lloyd (1862–1905) and Elizabeth Phoebe Key Lloyd (1868–1956). It should be noted that they were the great-grandchildren of Francis Scott Key, who is best known for writing a poem that became the lyrics for the United States' national

Wye House Plantation. *Library of Congress.*

anthem, "The Star-Spangled Banner." There is a recipe for caramel, written with childish penmanship and signed by Alicia in 1865. Alicia goes on to edit that caramel recipe three years later in 1868, when she would have been thirteen years old. Another recipe for preserving watermelon rind is attributed to McBlair in 1878.

As far as the various cookbook contributors, at least six different types of handwriting can be discerned throughout the pages. Many of the contributors appear to be friends or acquaintances, with at least twenty-one recipe contributors mentioned by name. Differing from the formal attributions given in these recipes, one scrap of paper tucked into the cookbooks is of special interest. It has four different recipes from three people, all with only first names attributed and with the name appearing in quotations. For example, the recipe for lemon cake is attributed to "Harriet" (cook). There is also "Harris" and "Dar Ellie," in comparison to the ladies who were designated by the title of "Mrs." or "Miss" followed by a surname for other recipes. It is likely that these three women who made the contributions to the Lloyd cookbook were African Americans. Since there is no date entered and the page was loose and tucked into the other bound cookbooks, there

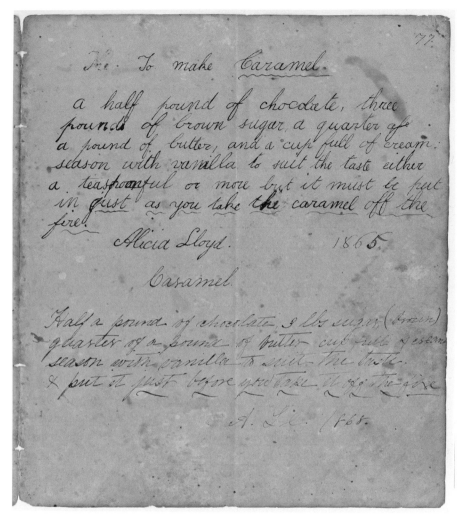

Above: Lloyd-Tilghman family cookbook. *University of Maryland–College Park.*

Opposite: Lloyd-Tilghman family cookbook recipes attributed to African American cooks. *University of Maryland–College Park.*

is no way to determine whether these people were enslaved or free African Americans at the time.

Traditional English recipes such as plum pudding, bread pudding, preserves, forcemeat balls and popovers were found in the Lloyd cookbooks. There were also non-English recipes such as gumbo soup, Indian meal muffins, sweet potato pie, rice and tomatoes, okra and hominy bread, which were definitely Native American and African in their origins. The cookbooks also have an abundance of fish and seafood recipes. There are at least sixteen different recipes to prepare seafood, with many of the recipes stipulating that any available or seasonal fish would serve as a suitable alternative.

The Lloyd family cookbooks also contain an excess of recipes for cakes, desserts and sweets. These signified the end of the meal or a dinner party and were the last thing guests would remember before leaving; thus, this was frequently a dish of pride, showcasing the hostess's skill. This was also probably the only dish that the Lloyd women would consistently prepare themselves instead of leaving the responsibility to the enslaved cooks.

OKRA AND TOMATO STEW

Serves 6 to 8

¼ cup unsalted butter
1 tablespoon olive oil
1 small onion, diced and dusted with flour
2 tablespoons finely chopped flat-leaf parsley
1 clove garlic, minced
1 sprig fresh thyme
Salt, to taste
Ground black pepper, to taste
⅛ teaspoon crushed red pepper flakes
4 cups vegetable chicken broth
3 cups vegetable broth
3½ cups fresh tomatoes, peeled and diced
2 cups fresh young okra, medium sliced
2 cups cooked rice

In a Dutch oven, heat the butter and oil on medium-low heat until the butter has melted. Add the onion and finely chopped parsley and gently cook until onion is translucent and soft. Add the garlic and cook for a minute more until fragrant.

Add the thyme, salt, black pepper and red pepper flakes and cook for another minute

Add the chicken broth, vegetable broth and tomatoes. Reduce the heat to a simmer and cook for 30 minutes.

Add the okra and cook for another 20 to 25 minutes, or until tender.

Taste and adjust the seasoning with salt and pepper, if needed.

To serve, add about ¼ cup cooked rice to a bowl and pour the soup over the rice.

Okra and tomato stew. *Author's collection.*

HARRIET'S LEMON POUND CAKE

Pound cakes are so named because originally they were made with one pound of butter, one pound of sugar, one pound of eggs and one pound of flour. This recipe is adapted from the recipe attributed to "Harriet" from the Lloyd family cookbooks (circa 1851–92).

Makes 1 Bundt cake

3 cups all-purpose flour
1 tablespoon baking powder
¾ teaspoon salt
1 cup unsalted butter, room temperature
½ cup shortening, room temperature
3 cups sugar
5 large eggs
1 cup whole milk
6 tablespoons lemon juice
1 lemon, ½ zested

For the glaze:
1 cup confectioners' sugar, plus more if needed
2 tablespoons fresh lemon juice

Preheat oven to 350 degrees Fahrenheit. Spray or butter and flour one large Bundt pan.

Sift flour, baking powder and salt into a medium bowl. Set aside.

Using an electric mixer, cream together butter, shortening and sugar. Add eggs one at a time, beating until well blended after each one.

Add dry ingredients in three additions to butter mixture alternately with milk, beginning and ending with flour mixture. Beat at low speed just until blended after each addition. Mix in lemon juice and zest.

Pour batter into the prepared pan. Bake the cake until tester inserted into center comes out clean, about 55 minutes. Cool the cake in the pan for 15 minutes. Turn the cake out onto racks and cool completely for about 1 hour.

When the cake is completely cool, carefully transfer it to a serving platter.

Lemon pound cake. *Марина Долбус. Adobe Stock Images.*

To make the glaze: in a medium bowl, whisk together the confectioners' sugar and lemon juice. Drizzle the glaze over the top of the cake with a spoon, letting it drip down the sides.

Serve the cake when ready.

PICKLED WATERMELON RIND

2 pounds watermelon rind, from a roughly 5-pound watermelon
1 cup apple cider vinegar
1 cup water
¾ cup sugar
¼ cup chopped candied or crystalized ginger
4 teaspoons kosher salt
1 teaspoon red pepper flake
1 teaspoon allspice berries
1 star anise pod

Special equipment:
1 sterilized 2-quart Mason jar with lid
Canning funnel

Using a sharp peeler, remove and discard the exterior green portion of the watermelon rind. You should now have rind that is mostly white, with a little bit of pink and/or red on one side. Cut into 1-inch cubes.

Add the apple cider vinegar, water, sugar, ginger, salt and spices to a 2-quart saucepan set over medium-high heat. Bring to a boil and hold for 1 minute, then carefully add the watermelon. Return to a boil and turn off the heat. Remove the pan from heat and cool for 30 minutes.

Move the pickles to a 2-quart jar using a canning funnel and ladle. Pour in as much of the pickling juice as possible.

Cover the jar and leave at room temperature for another 1½ hours.

Refrigerate overnight and consume within a month. These pickles must be refrigerated.

NELLY PARKE CUSTIS LEWIS

Eleanor "Nelly" Parke Custis Lewis (1779–1852) was the daughter of John Parke Custis and Eleanor Calvert Custis and the youngest of three granddaughters of Martha Dandridge Custis Washington by her marriage to Daniel Parke Custis. Following the premature death of her father in 1781 and her mother's remarriage to family friend Dr. David Stuart, Nelly and her brother George Washington Parke Custis were informally adopted by George and Martha Washington, and they were raised at Mount Vernon.

During George Washington's presidency, Nelly helped entertain guests at the first presidential mansion on Cherry Street in New York City, the second presidential mansion on Broadway in New York City and the third presidential mansion in Philadelphia.

Like her siblings, Nelly spent much of the remainder of her life keeping alive the memory of the beloved grandparents whom she described as "affectionate parents, whose loss can never be repair'd," and preserving the physical objects associated with their lives.

Years after Washington's death, Nelly gave an account of the first president's morning routine, which included getting up before sunrise, reading and writing until 7:00 a.m. in the summer or 7:30 a.m. in the winter and then eating "three small mush cakes (Indian meal) swimming in butter and honey, and drank three cups of tea without cream."

More than likely, Washington's first meal of the day was prepared by his enslaved chef, Hercules Posey. Washington's family loved Hercules's cooking; Washington's step-grandson George Washington Park Custis described Hercules as one of the best chefs in America. Washington praised Hercules's cooking so much that the president was reportedly angered and surprised when Hercules escaped and sought his own freedom.

HOECAKES AND HONEY

This recipe is a modern adaptation of the eighteenth-century original recipe found among the letters of Nelly Parke Custis Lewis, Washington's step-granddaughter.

Serves 4

> *2 cups stone-ground white cornmeal*
> *1½ to 2 cups lukewarm water*
> *1 package active dry yeast*
> *½ teaspoon salt*
> *1 large egg*
> *Lard, for frying*
> *Honey and butter, for serving*

The evening before, combine 1 cup of the cornmeal, 1½ cups of the lukewarm water and the yeast in a medium-size nonreactive or glass bowl. Whisk well; the mixture will be thin. Cover the bowl tightly with plastic wrap; let sit out overnight in a warm place.

The following morning, whisk in the remaining 1 cup cornmeal, salt and egg. Once again, cover the bowl tightly with plastic wrap; let it stand 15 to 20 minutes, allowing the just-added cornmeal to absorb some of the liquid and soften a little.

Check consistency; it should be close to a thin pancake batter, neither nearly liquid nor as thick as heavy cream. If needed, add a little more lukewarm water to the batter to achieve the right consistency.

Preheat the oven to 175 degrees Fahrenheit. Have a baking sheet ready to keep cooked hoecakes warm in the oven.

Begin heating a well-seasoned cast-iron skillet or griddle over medium-high heat. Apply a thin layer of lard using a moistened paper towel. Once skillet is hot, rub its interior quickly but thoroughly with the oiled towel.

Using a ladle, add the batter onto the griddle, using approximately ¼ cup for each hoecake. Cook until surface of hoecakes begins to bubble, 1 to 2 minutes. Using a spatula, carefully flip the cakes and cook until browned on the underside, 1 to 2 minutes more. Transfer to a baking sheet or platter; cover loosely with aluminum foil and keep warm in oven. Repeat, coating the skillet with more lard and cooking the remaining batter. Serve warm, with honey and butter, if desired.

Cook's Notes:
You can substitute vegetable oil or a vegetable spray for the lard.

Feel free to use assorted toppings, such as maple syrup, confectioners' sugar, jams, preserves, sweetened whipped cream or chocolate syrup for a modern twist.

VIRGINIA HAM BISCUITS

Since the colonial era in America, Virginia ham biscuits have always been a staple breakfast sandwich in the Mid-Atlantic. You can serve them for brunch, lunch or dinner or serve them as an appetizer at a tailgate party, a reception or just about any occasion that you can imagine. These simple, tasty sandwiches can be paired with a tangy mustard or jam, or both, for just the right taste of savory sweetness.

Makes about 40 mini sandwiches

> *2 cups all-purpose flour, plus more for dusting*
> *2 teaspoons double-acting baking powder*
> *½ teaspoon salt*
> *¼ cup cold lard*
> *1 cup milk*
> *Unsalted butter, for spreading on biscuits*
> *80 very thin slices Virginia ham (about 1 inch in diameter)*

> *Special equipment:*
> *Baking sheet, greased*

Preheat oven to 450 degrees Fahrenheit.

In a large bowl, sift together the flour, baking powder and salt.

Using a pastry blender, or two butter knives, blend in the lard, cutting it into bits, until the mixture resembles coarse meal.

Dust the work surface with a light coating of flour.

Stir in ¾ cup milk, or just enough to make a soft, pliable dough. Form the dough into a ball and roll or pat it out ½ inch thick on a floured surface. Cut out rounds with a 1-inch biscuit cutter or a small drinking glass dipped in flour and transfer them to the prepared greased baking sheet.

Repeat the process with the remaining scraps of dough by gently rolling into a ball and cutting the dough in the same manner and transferring the rounds to the baking sheet.

Brush the tops of the rounds lightly with milk and bake the biscuits in the middle of the oven for 10 to 12 minutes or until they are puffed and golden.

Remove the biscuits from the oven and allow them to cool on the racks. Using a serrated knife, split them, and if desired, spread them with unsalted butter. Arrange very thinly sliced ham on each biscuit. Replace the top of each biscuit and serve them as appetizers.

CHRISTOPHER LUDWIG

Christopher Ludwig (1720–1801) or Ludwick is known for three things: his skill at baking, his pepper pot stew and his generosity.

Christopher Ludwig was born in the small town of Giessen in Hesse-Darmstadt, Germany. Ludwig's father, Heinrich Ludwig, owned a successful bakeshop in the quaint settlement, where Ludwig began working at a young age. In 1732, Christopher's mother, Catherine Hiffle Ludwig, died. For two years following Catherine's death, Christopher accompanied his father to the family-owned bakery every day, developing his trade. At the age of fourteen, he began attending basic reading, writing and arithmetic classes at a local free school (Freischule). Also at this time, Ludwig received catechism lessons in the Lutheran Church, a denomination to which he remained faithful throughout his adult his life.

Very little else is known about Ludwig's formative years. However, he enlisted in the Austrian army and served in the Austro-Russian-Turkish War. He endured the hardships of a grueling seventeen-week-long battle known as the Siege of Prague, waged by the French under King Louis XV. When the French and Bavarians captured Prague in 1741, Ludwig and three thousand fellow Austrian soldiers were imprisoned. Ludwig was then conscripted into the Prussian army of Frederick II. When peace was finally declared in the summer of 1742, Ludwig received compensation for his services and was discharged from the Prussian army.

At this time, Ludwig decided to leave his homeland, and in 1742, he arrived in England and joined the British Royal Navy. His service records indicate that he served as a baker with the Royal British Navy aboard the HMS *Duke of Cumberland* from 1743 until 1745 and then served as a seaman in the merchant marine, sailing all over the world and gaining exposure to the lucrative business of oceanic trade. Ludwig first visited Philadelphia in 1749 and again in 1753. In the mid-eighteenth century, Philadelphia lacked quality pastry and confectionery shops, a business in which Ludwig possessed experience as well as a willingness to cultivate further skills. Ludwig returned to London and trained in the fine art of confectionery and gingerbread baking.

Traditionally, gingerbread had been produced and consumed in Europe for centuries. Reaching Western Europe during the Crusades, gingerbread consisted of the simple ingredients of flour, honey and spices. By the seventeenth century, English recipes replaced honey with treacle or molasses, largely due to its availability and cost, since it was manufactured in British West Indies sugarcane plantations. Most European bakers of the time produced gingerbread in soft loaf form, whereas the German bakers developed a recipe where the gingerbread was thinner and harder in cookie form. German soft loaves, known as *lebkuchen* ("bread of life"), were formed in large oval designs and sold to common citizens for everyday consumption.

The gingerbread cookies, however, were derived from small amounts of dough pressed between artistically crafted molds. Commonly, the finished products took the shape of royal figures or other human images, hence the development of the gingerbread man. Originally, bakers and confectionery shop owners decorated the gingerbread cookies with icing, as these cookies were reserved for special occasions such as carnivals or festivals. By the eighteenth century, gingerbread cookies in Europe had become even more popular among the masses as artists carved molds that reflected the lives of common people. Images included depictions of trades and professions, ordinary domestic activities, general proverbs, well-known political figures and religious symbols. As one historian has noted, eighteenth-century gingerbread molds provide insight into the daily lifestyle and popular culture of the era.

During the half decade prior to Ludwig's arrival, Philadelphia experienced a dramatic increase in European immigration. Ships delivered thousands of new immigrants to the city weekly. Many of these immigrants had undoubtedly enjoyed gingerbread in the German homelands and in other European nations during the height of its popularity. By capitalizing on the lack of gingerbread shops and bakeries in Philadelphia, in addition to the large influx of German immigrants in the city, Ludwig identified a market with a special interest in gingerbread.

Equipped with this new knowledge, Ludwig returned to Philadelphia the following year in 1754. Ultimately, he transferred the popularity of the gingerbread cookie from Europe to the American colony of Pennsylvania. He soon expanded his business as a gingerbread baker and confectioner located in Laetitia Court, where he amassed a great fortune.

From the very beginning, Ludwig was a staunch advocate of the American Revolution. In the summer of 1776, at the age of fifty-five, Ludwig enlisted as a volunteer. He was often invited to dine at George Washington's large dinner parties, and frequently their conversations were in relation to the bread supplies for the army. By 1777, Ludwig was appointed by the Continental Congress to the position of baker general to the American army.

On December 29, 1777, so the story goes, George Washington had spent ten days at Valley Forge, Pennsylvania, camped with his army and assorted

George Washington and Lafayette at Valley Forge. John Ward Dunsmore, 1907. *Library of Congress.*

women and children. The winter had been unremittingly harsh: up to a third of his forces were bootless—some had left bloody footprints in the snow as they marched into camp—and all were hungry. Local farmers were spurning the unreliable Revolutionary currency and selling their crops to the British. "Unless some great and capital change suddenly takes place," Washington wrote, "this Army must inevitably...Starve, dissolve, or disperse, in order to obtain subsistence in the best manner they can."

Legend has it that this desolate scene was supposedly improved when Ludwig improvised a version of pepper pot stew using tripe, vegetable scraps and whatever meager spices he had on hand. His goal was to "warm and strengthen the body of a soldier and inspire his flagging spirit," in Washington's words. Legend maintains that this brew revived the beleaguered army, sustaining it through its darkest months, and helped lead to its eventual victory.

By January 1781, the tribulations of war waged by an inefficient government began to adversely affect Ludwig. Since the spring of 1776,

Ludwig had endured four physically demanding years, in addition to incurring significant personal financial losses. As a result, Ludwig wrote to Congress on January 27, 1781, attempting to resign from his position as baker general. In his letter, Ludwig underscored the consequences of his dedication to the war, even mentioning the loss of his right eye. On February 14, 1781, the Board of War responded by not only refusing to accept Ludwig's resignation but also attempting to rectify his frustrations by providing the baker with additional compensation—ultimately only inflated Continental dollars—and the authority to hire added bakers. Ludwig faithfully remained with the army until the end of the war.

Ludwig spent a good deal of his later life in service to others. In 1793, the city of Philadelphia was hit hard by the yellow fever epidemic. Ludwig worked tirelessly at baking bread, gratuitously, to feed those who were sick or destitute. He was determined to help relieve the suffering of others.

Upon his death in 1801 at the age of eighty-one, Ludwig bequeathed $13,000 ($500,000 today) to fund a charitable trust "for the schooling and education gratis, of poor children of all denominations, in the city and liberties of Philadelphia, without exception to the country, extraction, or religious principles of their parents or friends." The trust has grown to almost $5 million, and grants amounting to somewhat over $200,000 are awarded each year.

Funds were also awarded to several different organizations in the city of Philadelphia. Organizations such as the immigrant aid society Deutsche Gesellschaft von Pennsylvanien, the University of Pennsylvania and two church charities for poor children received money from the Christopher Ludwig estate.

The remainder of the estate was given to create a free school. In 1872, that school was named in his honor as the Ludwig Institute, which evolved into the Christopher Ludwig Foundation in 1995. The Christopher Ludwig Foundation serves as a charitable corporation with its own trustees and endowment. For over two centuries, the trustees have fulfilled Christopher Ludwig's mandate, and the group remains active in its mission to the present day.

PHILADELPHIA PEPPER POT STEW

The culinary origins of Philadelphia pepper pot stew can be found in West Africa, as the recipe crossed the Atlantic Ocean during the Middle Passage with African slaves landing on the shores of the British West Indies. Versions of the recipe eventually traveled up the Atlantic coast of North America, where a version eventually became a signature dish of Philadelphia, the City of Brotherly Love.

The Philadelphia pepper pot also represents German influence, as German immigrants changed the recipe to include the use of meats such as beef tripe and veal knuckle, which were common in Europe. The rich, spicy stew became a staple in Philly, where West Indian hawkers advertised it with cries of "pepper pot, smoking hot!" Legend has it that Philadelphia pepper pot was the stew that saved the Continental army during the American Revolutionary War.

Pepper pot stew became as iconic as other beloved Philadelphia foods such as cheesesteak, scrapple, hoagies and water ice and took center stage. In 1811, the popular German American artist John Lewis Krimmel (1786–1821) was exhibiting his work Pepper Pot: A Scene in the Philadelphia Market, *in which an African American woman ladles the popular stew and sells it to a crowd of customers. Andy Warhol's (1928–1987)* Small Torn Campbell Soup Can (Pepper Pot), *a famous 1962 painting from his Campbell Soup Series, sold for almost $12 million in 2016. The Philadelphia chapter of the Public Relations Society of America even began using the pepper pot as the symbol for its annual awards in 1968.*

But unlike the other iconic dishes of the city, Philadelphia pepper pot has waned in popularity and is now merely a curio in a few Philadelphia restaurants and among die-hard foodie fans of American colonial cuisine. The famous City Tavern in Philadelphia still features a West Indian version of the stew on its lunch menu. Given its long culinary journey, Philadelphia pepper pot still retains something of the frugality and hardship that enslaved Africans and soldiers of the American Revolutionary War endured, as it literally become a soup that represents the "melting pot" of America.

Serves 8 to 10

1 ½ pounds cleaned, precooked honeycomb tripe
12 ounces pork shoulder
12 ounces beef shoulder
Kosher salt, to taste
2 tablespoons canola oil
4 cloves garlic, finely chopped
2 carrots, large diced
2 celery stalks, diced
1 medium white onion, roughly chopped
¼ Scotch Bonnet or habanero chile, stemmed, seeded and chopped
1 pound yams, or a mix of plantains, taro root, cassava and white potatoes,
peeled and cut into ¼-inch cubes
1 cup chopped scallions
1 veal knuckle
16 cups beef stock
1 tablespoon freshly ground allspice
1 tablespoon freshly ground black pepper, plus more to taste
1 teaspoon fresh thyme, chopped
2 bay leaves
1 pound collard greens, rinsed and chopped
½ pound turnip greens
½ cup spinach
¼ bunch fresh parsley, chopped, for garnish
Slices of crusty bread, for serving

Wash the tripe well in cold water. Place it in a large saucepan and cover with cold water. Bring the saucepan to a boil and then reduce the heat and simmer the tripe for 20 minutes. Using a colander, drain the tripe; leave to cool in a shallow bowl, then chop into small cubes and set aside, covered.

Place the pork and beef in a bowl; rub heavily with salt. Cover with a clean dish towel and let sit at room temperature for 1 hour. Rinse meat, dry with paper towels and cut into ¼-inch cubes.

Pepper pot stew. *Author's collection.*

Heat oil in a large Dutch oven or an 8-quart saucepan over medium-high heat. Working in batches, add pork and beef and cook until browned, about 10 minutes.

Add garlic, carrots, celery, onion and Scotch Bonnet or habanero; cook until soft, about 10 minutes. Add the yams (or taro, cassava, potato or plantain) and scallions; cook until the yams begin to soften, about 5 minutes. Return the tripe to the pan with the veal knuckle. Add stock, allspice, pepper, thyme and bay leaves; bring the pot to a rolling boil. Reduce heat to medium-high. Using a chilled metal spoon, remove any scum that forms on the surface the surface. Simmer the stew until the meat and yams are tender, about 1 to 2½ hours. Add collard greens, turnip greens and spinach and cook until wilted, about 10 minutes.

Remove the veal knuckle and allow to cool, then remove the meat from the bone. Roughly chop the meat and return it to the saucepan to warm through. Taste and adjust the seasoning with salt and black pepper as needed.

Ladle the soup into hot bowls and garnish with chopped parsley. Serve with crusty bread.

Cook's Note:
Tripe is commonly available in most supermarkets throughout the United States. You can also purchase it from a local butcher to guarantee freshness. There are also a few online specialty markets that sell tripe by the pound for a reasonable price.

GINGERBREAD CAKE WITH SPICE WHIPPED CREAM

Gingerbread was a popular dessert during the Christmas holidays in colonial America. This modern adaption of a classic recipe has been enhanced with a spiced whipped cream with just a touch of honey and cardamom.

Serves 9

For the gingerbread:
9 tablespoons unsalted butter, softened
⅓ cup granulated white sugar
1 cup molasses
1 large egg
2¼ cups all-purpose flour
1 teaspoon baking soda
1 teaspoon ground ginger
1 teaspoon ground cinnamon
¼ teaspoon salt
¾ cup water

For the spiced whipped cream:
⅛ teaspoon cardamom
1 cup heavy cream
1 tablespoon honey

Preheat the oven to 325 degrees Fahrenheit.

In a large bowl, cream butter and sugar until light and fluffy. Beat in molasses and egg until well blended. In another bowl, whisk together the flour, baking soda, ginger, cinnamon and salt; add to creamed mixture alternately with water.

Transfer the batter to a greased 9x9-inch baking pan. Bake for 35 to 40 minutes or until a wooden toothpick inserted in the center comes out clean. Remove from the oven and place on a wire rack to cool.

Meanwhile, in a medium bowl, whip cardamom, heavy cream and honey until firm peaks form.

To serve, cut the cake into 9 squares and serve warmed. Top with the spiced whipped cream.

JAMES HEMINGS

Macaroni and cheese. Three simple words for a dish with such a complex history. This particular dish has become a classic if not the quintessential American food to grace dinner tables since the colonial era. But where did it come from? Who "invented" it? And last but not least, how did it become one of the most beloved comfort foods of all time?

The first modern recipe for the dish was included in *The Experienced French Housekeeper* by Elizabeth Raffald (1769). Raffald's recipe is for a bechamel sauce with cheddar cheese, which is mixed with macaroni, sprinkled with parmesan and baked until bubbly and golden.

From 1769, macaroni and cheese grew in popularity across Europe. It is likely that the classic American macaroni and cheese returned with Thomas Jefferson to Virginia after his sojourn in Italy. Jefferson brought back a pasta machine from Italy in 1793. James Hemings, a slave owned by Jefferson, was among the first chefs in America to serve macaroni and cheese.

The story of James Hemings (1765–1801) is a fascinating one, as told by Madison Hemings, his nephew. James was one of twelve children of Elizabeth "Betty" Hemings (1735–1807). Betty was the "property" of John Wayles, "a Welchman." Betty became Wayles's slave concubine sometime following the death of his third wife. James was the second oldest of the six children that union was said to have produced. John Wayles was also the father of Thomas Jefferson's wife, Martha, through his first marriage to Martha Eppes. Thus, Martha Jefferson was the half sister of James and his five full siblings, including Sally Hemings. Upon Wayles's death in 1773, Jefferson inherited through his wife 135 slaves, including Betty Hemings and her children. James Hemings became the property of Thomas Jefferson in January 1774. He was nine years old at that time. Later that year, James and his brother Robert were taken to Monticello. Known also as Jemmy, Jim, Jamey and Jame, this young slave would grow up serving Jefferson as house servant, messenger, driver, traveling attendant and eventually chef.

Perhaps the most rewarding time of James's service began in 1784, when Jefferson was appointed minister plenipotentiary in Paris by Congress. Together with John Adams and Benjamin Franklin, Jefferson had the responsibility of negotiating treaties of amity and commerce with European countries. On the same day Jefferson assumed his diplomatic role, he wrote to his future secretary William Short that he wished to take his servant James with him to France "for a particular purpose": to have James trained in the art of French cookery.

Left: Thomas Jefferson (1743–1826). *White House Historical Association.*

Below: Monticello, the home of Thomas Jefferson. *Wikimedia Commons.*

So why was Jefferson obsessed with French cuisine? Classical French cuisine evolved in the early seventeenth century as a new idiom for conspicuous consumption among French aristocrats. It replaced a Renaissance cooking tradition that emphasized layering multiple flavors and the lavish use of exotic and costly spices like cinnamon, nutmeg and ginger. As spice prices declined in the early seventeenth century—the result of the same improvements in European naval and military technology that fueled colonial expansion—elite diners required effective ways to signal wealth. The new French cuisine aimed for *le vrai gout*, meaning "the true taste"—preparations that required great technical skill and highlighted the natural flavors of the main ingredients, revealing their freshness and quality. It emphasized fresh vegetables and fruits that were perishable and fragile and sparked costly investments in new varieties, cultivation techniques and vegetable gardens.

James was nineteen years old when he sailed from Boston with Jefferson. The travelers arrived in Paris on August 6, 1784. James was apprenticed to a *traiteur* (caterer) named Combeaux who provided Jefferson's meals during the first year of his stay in Paris. He subsequently trained under Jefferson's female cook and also a pastry chef, as well as with a chef of the Prince de Condé. James learned quickly and in 1787 became the chef de cuisine at the Hôtel de Langeac, which was Jefferson's private residence on the Champs-Élysées.

Jefferson's ongoing investments in French kitchen technology, French training for Hemings and building and maintaining a massive vegetable garden stocked with exotic varieties all make sense only when we see them as part of this larger historical process as Indigenous, African and European cultures began to forge new food pathways in the Mid-Atlantic.

James Hemings was freed by Jefferson in 1796 on the condition that James would train his younger brother Robert to replace him as chef in the Jefferson household. Sadly, James died at the age of thirty-six. His only material legacy was an inventory of kitchen utensils and four recipes. Hemings's considerable and historic influences on American food and culture—including the introduction of macaroni and cheese, ice cream, whipped cream and French fries—have long been attributed to Thomas Jefferson. For the most part, Jefferson has been wrongly credited with creating these dishes, which were actually Hemings's genius adaptations of French haute cuisine. Despite Hemings's contributions to the culinary world, sadly, there are no written reminiscences from this intelligent, literate man himself, in his own hand.

James Hemings's deed of manumission. *Library of Congress.*

Deed of Manumission for James Hemings, 5 February 1796
This indenture made at Monticello in the county of Albemarle and commonwealth of
Virginia on the fifth day of February one thousand seven hundred and ninety six witnesseth
that I Thomas Jefferson of Monticello aforesaid do emancipate, manumit and make free
James Hemings, son of Betty Hemings, which said James is now of the age of thirty years
so that in future he shall be free and of free condition, and discharged of all duties and
claims of servitude whatsoever, and shall have all the rights and privileges of a freedman.
In witness whereof I have hereto set my hand and seal on the day and year abovewritten,
and have made these presents double of the same date, tenor and indenture one whereof is
lodged in the court of Albemarle aforesaid to be recorded, and the other is delivered by me
to the said James Hemings to be produced when and where it may be necessary.
Th: Jefferson

Signed, sealed and delivered in presence of
John Carr
Francis Anderson

In 1802, Jefferson served a "macaroni pie" at a state dinner, more than
likely prepared from a recipe by James Hemings and cooked by his brother
Robert. Since that time, the dish has been associated with the United States.

A recipe called "macaroni and cheese" appeared in the 1824 cookbook
The Virginia Housewife, written by Mary Randolph. Born in 1762 at Ampthill
Plantation in Chesterfield County, Virginia, Mary was the daughter of
Thomas Mann Randolph Sr. (1741–1794) and Anne Cary Randolph

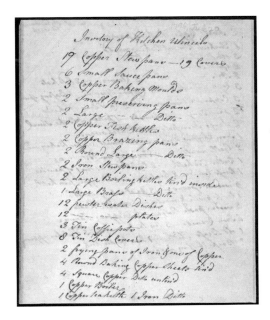

James was a member of the Hemings family inherited by Jefferson and his wife at the death of his father-in-law, John Wayles. James, the son of Elizabeth Hemings and, most probably, Jefferson's father-in-law, had been trained as a French chef. This was the final accounting inventory of Monticello kitchen utensils and equipment prepared and written by James Hemings just two weeks after Jefferson honored the written promise of freedom he had made to James in 1793. *Library of Congress.*

(1745–1789). The extended Randolph family was one of the richest and most politically significant in eighteenth-century Virginia. Mary's father was orphaned at a young age and raised by Thomas Jefferson's parents, who were distant cousins. Her father also served in the Virginia House of Burgesses, the Revolutionary conventions of 1775 and 1776 and the Virginia state legislature. She was also a cousin of Mary Lee Fitzhugh Custis, the wife of George Washington Parke Custis (grandson of Martha Washington and step-grandson of George Washington) and the godmother of his daughter Mary Randolph Custis, who married Robert E. Lee. It is believed that Randolph's recipe may have been one of James Hemings's creations. It had three ingredients: macaroni, cheese and butter, layered together and baked in an oven. The cookbook was the most influential one of the nineteenth century.

Similar recipes for macaroni and cheese appear in the 1852 *Hand-book of Useful Arts* and the 1861 *Godey's Lady's Book.*

By the mid-1880s, cookbooks as far west as Kansas included recipes for macaroni and cheese casseroles. Factory production of the main ingredients made the dish affordable and recipes made it accessible, and macaroni and cheese lost its upper-class appeal. Fashionable restaurants in New York ceased to serve it.

The familiar blue box was introduced to the American public in 1937, at the end of the Great Depression. It was called "the housewife's best friend, a nourishing one pot meal," because it was a fast, filling and inexpensive way to feed a family. In that year alone, more than eight million boxes were sold, and the popularity of the Kraft box dinners continues today mainly because every American child has grown up with macaroni and cheese.

Over the years, every home cook has had homemade recipes that include pasta, butter or cream and Parmesan cheese. American cooks often improvised, using cheddar, Colby or more affordable processed cheeses and spices like nutmeg and mustard. Today, gourmet versions call for a variety of cheeses, including Gruyère, smoked Gouda, Monterey Jack, Havarti and goat, and add-ins like bacon, tomatoes, shallots and even truffles.

TRUFFLED LOBSTER MACARONI AND CHEESE

This is the perfect dish for when you want to indulge and eat like royalty! This dish is filled with succulent chunks of lobster meat and black truffle butter and packed with an assortment of cheeses. It's the pinnacle of elevated comfort food—sophisticated, yet laidback. A grown-up mac 'n' cheese!

Serves 6 to 8

2 cups water
2 cups chicken broth
1 pound dried macaroni pasta
2 tablespoons olive oil
½ cup chopped white onion
2 medium leeks, thinly sliced
½ teaspoon fresh thyme leaves
1 pound cooked lobster meat, chopped
8 ounces Gruyère cheese, cubed
½ cup Mozzarella cheese, cubed
⅓ cup Fontina cheese, cubed
⅓ cup grated Parmesan cheese
⅓ cup smoked Gouda cheese, cubed
½ cup heavy cream
½ cup black truffle butter
Salt, to taste
⅛ teaspoon ground white pepper
⅛ teaspoon cayenne pepper
¼ cup chopped fresh parsley
All-purpose flour, if needed

Preheat oven to 350 degrees Fahrenheit. Grease a 3-quart baking dish and set aside.

In a large stockpot, bring the water and chicken broth to a boil. Add the pasta to the boiling liquids and cook 12 to 15 minutes, or to desired tenderness. Drain pasta, return to the same pot and set aside.

Truffled lobster macaroni and cheese. *Author's collection.*

Meanwhile, add the oil to a large skillet and heat on medium heat. Add the onions, leeks, thyme and a pinch of salt and cook for about 5 minutes or until the onions are translucent and the leeks are tender. Remove from heat and set aside.

Heat a large saucepan over medium heat and add the cooked pasta. Stir in the onion and leek mixture, lobster meat, cheeses, heavy cream, truffle butter, salt, white pepper, cayenne pepper and parsley into the cooked pasta. If the mixture is loose or too soupy, stir in the flour. Stir gently and transfer the mixture to the prepared baking dish.

Bake, covered, for 20 minutes, or until mixture is heated through. Let stand for 10 minutes before serving.

MARINATED ASPARAGUS

Asparagus became widely available in America during colonial times and was a particular favorite of Thomas Jefferson. Given Jefferson's preference for vegetable-based cuisine and his love of French food, he had a square in his Monticello garden reserved just for asparagus. It was one of the few vegetables for which he documented its cultivation, and he recorded its seasonal arrival at his Monticello table twenty-two times, usually in early April. Given how much asparagus grew in the gardens at Monticello, James Hemings may very well have prepared asparagus this way for Jefferson and his dinner guests.

This colonial dish is still being served at the City Tavern restaurant in Philadelphia. The City Tavern opened in 1773 and played host to the founding fathers of the United States and was the unofficial meeting place of the First Continental Congress. It was also the site of several victory parties of the Continental army led by George Washington. Other high-profile events took place at the City Tavern, including the first-anniversary celebration of the Fourth of July. The original City Tavern structure was destroyed in a fire and demolished in 1854. In 1948, Congress commissioned a historically accurate reconstruction of the building on the original construction site. The City Tavern reopened in 1976. Items on the menu are still being prepared at the Tavern in the traditional colonial style. Make sure you make a reservation to get a taste of history at this iconic restaurant.

Serves 4

1 ½ pounds green asparagus
2 tablespoons red wine vinegar
½ cup olive oil
Pinch of fresh thyme
Pinch of chopped fresh parsley
1 egg, hard cooked and chopped
½ small red onion, finely chopped
1 tablespoon capers, drained
Salt, to taste
Freshly ground white pepper, to taste

1800 newspaper advertisement for the City Tavern. *New York City Public Library.*

Wash the asparagus. Peel and trim the tough ends of the stalks. In a large saucepan, bring 2 quarts of lightly salted water to a boil over high heat. Place the asparagus in the water and cook until just tender, 2 to 3 minutes.

Drain asparagus. Plunge the asparagus into an ice bath to stop the cooking process. Let stand about 5 minutes, until the asparagus is cool. Drain the asparagus again and pat the asparagus dry with paper towels. Set aside.

In a medium-size mixing bowl, whisk together the vinegar, oil, thyme, parsley, egg, onion and capers and salt and pepper to taste.

Place the asparagus on a serving platter. Pour the vinaigrette evenly over the asparagus. Let the asparagus marinate in the dressing for a few minutes (optional). Garnish with additional chopped egg and parsley, if desired. Serve immediately at room temperature.

SNOW EGGS

Oeufs à la neige, or "snow eggs," are a classic French dessert of poached meringues floating in a custard sauce. A recipe for snow eggs can be found in the Thomas Jefferson Archives at Monticello. This recipe is a modern adaptation of a recipe from the nineteenth century.

Serves 8

For the meringues:
4 eggs
Tiny pinch of salt (about 1/16 teaspoon)
¾ cup sugar, divided
1½ teaspoons vanilla extract, divided
2½ cups milk, plus up to 1 cup more

For the chocolate sauce:
2 ounces fine-quality bittersweet chocolate (not unsweetened), finely chopped

Separate the eggs and set the yolks aside.

Put egg whites into a copper bowl, if you have one, but any large bowl will do. Feel free to use a standing mixer with a whisk attachment, if you like. Beat eggs with a large balloon whisk, if you have one, but any whisk will work, or in the machine until foamy.

Add salt and keep beating as it turns fluffy. Keep beating until firm peaks form—when you lift the whisk or beaters out of the egg whites, the peak that forms should droop a bit but then stay put.

Fold in ¼ cup of the sugar, incorporating 1 tablespoon at a time. Then fold in ½ teaspoon of the vanilla.

Put 2½ cups milk and ¼ cup sugar in a wide pot or sauté pan. Heat the milk to a gentle simmer, stirring occasionally to help the sugar melt.

Using an oval-shaped soupspoon, form 8 meringue "eggs" by scooping the mixture with one spoon and shaping it in that spoon with the other spoon. Then use the free spoon to gently help ease the meringue into the simmering milk. Do as many meringues as fit without crowding or touching too much in the pan. Poach meringues until set on bottom, about 2 minutes, then carefully turn over and poach until set throughout, until the meringues are firm, about 2 minutes more.

When the meringues are cooked, lift them out of the milk using a slotted spoon and drain them on a clean kitchen towel. Repeat with remaining egg white mixture.

To make the custard:
When all meringues are cooked, strain the poaching milk through a fine-mesh sieve into a very large measuring cup. Add more milk to equal 2 cups, if necessary.

In a small bowl, whisk the egg yolks with the remaining ¼ cup sugar and a pinch of salt in a 2-quart heavy saucepan until light yellow and thick. Keep whisking as you pour the milk mixture, which will still be very warm, into the egg yolks. Constant whisking will keep the yolks from curdling.

Transfer this mixture to a medium saucepan and cook over low heat, stirring constantly with a wooden spoon until the mixture thickens enough to coat the back of the spoon and registers 170 to 175 degrees Fahrenheit on an instant-read thermometer. Using your finger, pass through the sauce on the back of the spoon and have a taste. If a path remains, the custard is ready.

Stir in the remaining teaspoon of vanilla. Strain custard sauce, if you like.

Cover everything with plastic wrap and chill it up to a day before you serve, or prepare the dishes, cover them and chill them until you serve them, or assemble the desserts and eat them warm.

To assemble the dessert:
Melt chocolate in a small metal bowl set over a small saucepan of barely simmering water, stirring occasionally, until smooth.

Put less than ¼ cup of the sauce in shallow bowls or rimmed plates and arrange three meringues on top of the custard. Drizzle the chocolate sauce over the meringues and serve.

Elizabeth Goodfellow

She was married and widowed three times, and her full name was Elizabeth Baker Pearson Coane Goodfellow (circa 1767–1851), but history has recorded her as Elizabeth Goodfellow or Betsy Goodfellow, who was "justly-celebrated" during her lifetime throughout the city of Philadelphia as a renowned baker, confectioner and founder of a cooking school. But somehow, through the passage of time, she was almost forgotten. Elizabeth Goodfellow did not leave behind any personal records or even write a cookbook. Culinary historian Becky Diamond has assembled the many parts of the puzzle that was Goodfellow's life from old recipe books, advertisements, letters, diaries, genealogical records, firsthand accounts and other primary sources.

In Philadelphia during the first decades of the nineteenth century, Elizabeth Goodfellow ran a popular bakery and sweet shop. Very little is known about her personal life. By 1801, she was married and conducting business on Dock Street, Philadelphia, as Elizabeth Pearson, pastry cook. Her daughter, Sarah Anne Pearson Bouvier (1800–1826), had been born the year before. She and her second husband, Robert Coane, had a son, Robert Coane Jr. (1804–1877), who would become a partner in his mother's bakery and catering business in 1837. Lastly, by the time she was forty years of age, in 1808, she had married William Goodfellow, a clockmaker, but he died ten years later.

Mrs. Goodfellow is known to have made the first commercially sold lemon meringue pie in America. Her queen cakes, Spanish buns and coconut pies were locally renowned as well. She also had a reputation for training her workers in the preeminent art of cooking. In 1843, a rival Philadelphia baker advertised for "a journeyman baker," stating that "one who served time with Parkinson or Mrs. Goodfellow would be preferred." In addition to catering to Philadelphia's wealthy families and a reputation for having the finest desserts and sweet dishes in the young country, her business stood out from every other establishment in another way: she ran a small school to teach the art of cooking to wealthy young ladies, the first of its kind in America.

She was also an advocate for regional foods that we now think of as completely American, such as Indian (corn) meal, tomatoes, squash— things that were grown here in the New World that could be incorporated into the Old World recipes. Her students also recalled that she stressed using simple, wholesome ingredients that were locally grown nearly two hundred

Frontispiece engraving of author Eliza Leslie from *Godey's Lady's Book,* 1846. *Wikipedia.*

years ago, presaging today's modern home cooks and professional chefs' obsession with fresh, local ingredients and produce. For some culinary historians, Goodfellow became the woman who changed the way Americans learned how to structure menus and prepare meals. But that is a matter that is up for debate.

Despite her fame—references to her cooking as a benchmark abound in the literature of the period—we know very little about who she was. Goodfellow owned a baked goods and confectionery shop for over fifty years to support herself and her children. In the U.S. census records, she is listed with her son Robert and his family as residing "over the shop" at 71 South Sixth Street, with many young workers lodging with them. According to her obituary, Elizabeth Goodfellow died on January 5, 1851, at age eighty-three in Philadelphia, and the funeral services were to be held at Robert Coane's home.

Since Goodfellow never published any of her recipes, culinary historians have had to rely on her students, most notably Eliza Leslie (1787–1858), who recorded many of Goodfellow's creations and techniques. Leslie would gain fame and financial security by publishing Goodfellow's recipes as the foundation for her first cookbook, *Seventy-Five Receipts for Pastry, Cakes, and Sweetmeats,* in 1828, where Leslie followed Goodfellow's recipe layout by putting the ingredients first rather than in the usual paragraph format. The cookbook was a success and became extremely popular, as it went through eleven editions until 1839.

Susan Israel (1790–1845), the daughter of Revolutionary War general Joseph Israel from Delaware, was also a student of Goodfellow's cooking school, where she "graduated with honors" in 1807. She married Thomas Painter in 1811. Her family had "widespread appreciation of her recipes, all of which have been carefully preserved." Many recipes from her handwritten cookbook were included in *Colonial Receipt Book: Celebrated Old Receipts Used a Century Ago by Mrs. Goodfellow's Cooking School*; however, some recipes were added after her 1807 class, such as Delmonico pudding and mountain cake.

Goodfellow's recipes, such as sweet potato pudding, floating island, Swiss cream, boiled custard, dove pudding, apple pudding, potato pudding, white potato pie, Oxford pudding, puff paste, mince pies, queen cake, cream cake, plum cake, nut cake, coconut cake, rose jumble, yeast cake, drop cake, potato biscuit, Barrington rusk, waffles, preserved citron, cookies and hickory-nut macaroons, can also be found in two books submitted by a few of her students' descendants and compiled in 1907.

MRS. GOODFELLOW'S DOVER CAKE

Makes 1 Cake

Bread crumbs for coating pan
2 sticks unsalted butter, at room temperature
½ teaspoon salt
2 cups sugar
8 large eggs
¼ cup brandy
¼ cup dry Madeira or sherry
1 tablespoon orange blossom water
2¾ cups rice flour, spooned into a cup and leveled
Confectioners' sugar, for dusting

Adjust an oven rack to the lower third position and preheat the oven to 325 degrees Fahrenheit.

Butter a 10-inch Bundt pan or coat with cooking spray and dust the inside with fine bread crumbs; knock out the excess and set aside.

Beat the butter in a large bowl with an electric mixer on medium speed until smooth and creamy, about 1 minute. Add the salt and ¼ cup of the sugar and beat for 20 to 30 seconds. Beat in the remaining 1½ cups sugar ¼ cup at a time, beating for 20 to 30 seconds after each addition. Beat on medium-high speed for 5 minutes. Beat in the eggs one at a time, beating for 1 minute after each addition.

Combine the brandy, Madeira or sherry and orange blossom water in a measuring cup. On low speed, add the rice flour to the butter mixture in 3 additions, alternating with the liquid, beginning and ending with the rice flour and beating only until each addition is incorporated. Scrape the batter into the prepared pan and smooth the top.

Bake for 50 to 55 minutes, until the cake is golden brown and springs back when gently pressed and a toothpick inserted into the thickest part comes out clean. Cool in the pan for 20 minutes. Cover with a wire rack and invert. Remove the pan and cool the cake completely.

Transfer the cake to a cake plate. Just before serving, dust with confectioners' sugar.

To serve, cut into thin slices with a serrated knife.

CHAPTER 5

The Road to Freedom

African Americans in the Food Industry

THE BLACK WATERMEN OF THE CHESAPEAKE

Indigenous communities dating back thousands of years have relied on the harvests of fish and shellfish for survival. Commercial fishing has occurred in Maryland for more than four hundred years. Oystering, crabbing, fishing, sailing, boat building and net making were ancient skills that were used along the coastal settlements of Africa. Work on the water has a long tradition among Africans and African Americans along the port cities of Baltimore, New York, Delaware and Philadelphia. Early records show millions of pounds of Atlantic menhaden, rockfish, shad and oysters being harvested every year. The commercial fishing industry rapidly expanded in the nineteenth century, with annual landings of as much as forty-eight million pounds of shad and millions of bushels of oysters. In reviewing the history of watermen, African Americans were crucial to the evolution and continuation of maritime industries. Most of their names were lost to history, buried in old census records and "colored directories." Their stories were not told in coffee table books celebrating the Chesapeake Bay's maritime tradition. If they were known at all, they were known as crab pickers and deckhands, not as business owners and union leaders and masters of their own fates. African Americans who escaped slavery by sailing up the Bay to freedom were also among the people who built the great ships that roamed the world from the port of Baltimore. They also served as captains on fishing vessels and oyster boats sailing the Mid-Atlantic.

In colonial times, tobacco was the mainstay of the economies of Maryland and Virginia. Many of the workers at tobacco plantations were slaves or indentured servants from Africa and Europe. Plantations were often located along the Chesapeake's rivers, where soil quality was better and the tobacco could be transported via local waterways. When the slave-driven plantation economy collapsed, Chesapeake's tobacco and agricultural industries began to decline at the end of the eighteenth century due to low tobacco prices and worn-out soil. A majority of the plantation owners forced their slaves to work on fishing boats. Evidence of the change in the economy can be found in surviving documents such as old family wills, inventories and bills of sale in county courthouses along the Bay, where the names of slaves and their occupations are listed. Other slave owners profited once again by slave labor by demanding that their slaves had to buy their own freedom, and many did so "with a small boat and a pair of oyster tongs and a lot of hard work." Free African Americans also turned to the water to make a living, ultimately helping the region's economy and cultural history flourish.

Throughout the mid-1800s, the rivers and tributaries of the Chesapeake Bay were important pathways along the Underground Railroad. Published narratives by escaped slaves revealed a network of creeks and rivers leading north to Pennsylvania and New Jersey and desolate marshes full of hiding places. In a vain attempt to stop the escapes, the Maryland General Assembly passed a law in 1836 requiring that all large boats be captained by white people. "A clandestine trade was carried on, and slaves had found facilities for running away," as the legislators stated in 1836 in the law's preamble.

Meanwhile, Black sailors were a common sight on the streets of Baltimore. The great statesman, author, orator and abolitionist Frederick Douglass, born into slavery on the Eastern Shore, escaped to freedom simply by borrowing a sailor's uniform and boarding a train, unchallenged, to Philadelphia.

The history of Fells Point in Baltimore is filled with the immigrant experience—mostly from Germany and Eastern Europe. In an 1819 Baltimore directory, there is a listing for dozens of sailors and shipyard workers. Their names were marked with daggers to indicate they were Black. Most of the African Americans, both free and enslaved, worked as ship's caulkers, which was the most highly paid and most skilled job after ship's carpenter. Even Frederick Douglass worked as a caulker in Baltimore's shipyards, earning wages as a slave. After the Civil War, newly emancipated slaves found their way to the Chesapeake's shores, where they helped build the region's economy and shape its culture. By 1871, the "colored directory" of Baltimore listed men and women working in thirty-five maritime occupations.

By the 1860s, the Chesapeake Bay was the United States' primary source of oysters, which created an industry in need of strong labor. The availability of jobs and relatively low start-up costs for new watermen lured many newly freed Black people to the region. There were opportunities for Black watermen to make a living shucking oysters, processing seafood and even building boats for the industry. New African American communities formed along the Bay's shores, creating cultural and economic centers in the area. Their traditions, which survived the Middle Passage, became part of the local fishing industry, and many of them still exist today.

Many African Americans began by "sharecropping the sea"—captaining skipjacks owned by whites—and eventually, through earning a livelihood, many earned enough to purchase their own boats. It was grueling work, but it offered opportunities that did not exist on shore.

During the early 1900s, it was not uncommon to hear men singing while hauling in seines full of fish. These rhythmic songs, known as chanteys, are rooted in African tradition. Chanteys helped the men coordinate their movements and control the pace of the labor-intensive work. Many watermen believed that singing chanteys helped them haul in nets faster and more efficiently than those who did not sing.

The waterman had his own independence by being self-employed, whereas other people worked as laborers, crab pickers or servants who depended on other people for their livelihood. The waterman wasn't beholden to anyone, but the struggle for independence often lasted decades and exacted a brutal price. African American watermen often faced troubles more insidious than bad weather. In the 1940s, 1950s and 1960s, when the fishing industry was

Lithograph titled *Crab Pickers in St. Michael's,* by Ruth Star Rose, 1932. *Chesapeake Bay Maritime Museum.*

Unknown oysterman. *Chesapeake Bay Maritime Museum.*

booming, there were plenty of fish but not enough ice. "There'd be a line at the dock, and the black guys would have to go to the end of the line. The ice would melt and the longer the fish sat, the more the price went down. Some of the guys have told me they'd take their oysters back out and dump them rather than sell them for peanuts," related Vincent Leggett, author and founder of the Blacks of the Chesapeake Bay, which works to share the legacy of African American achievement in the Bay's seafood and maritime industries and foster environmental stewardship.

"Fair wages for a fair day's work!" was the motto of the Black Waterman's Union, formed in 1941 by Crisfield waterman Elbert Bell and others. The union lasted more than thirty years, but the Bay's dwindling harvest and the advent of the crab-picking machine eventually led to its demise.

Although Black watermen in southern Anne Arundel County numbered about three hundred in the mid-twentieth century, their ranks have dwindled significantly in recent years. Today, about fifteen African American watermen still ply their trade on the Chesapeake waterways or make their livings in related businesses, such as marine engine repair, boat repair or boat building. Some even make a living by providing fishing excursions for local tourists.

CODDIES

A 1941 newspaper advertisement for
Cohen's Coddies, re-created from the
Baltimore Sun. Author's collection.

The origins of coddies can be traced back to the 1800s, when it was a popular food among African American slaves along the Mid-Atlantic coast. It closely resembles the codfish cakes that have been found in Jamaica even to this day. Coddies did not become available commercially until a Jewish merchant by the name of Louis Cohen and his wife, Fannie Jacobson Cohen, began selling them from a Bel Air market ice cream stand in Baltimore around 1910. Their enterprise was so successful that they soon established a coddie factory. The Cohens eventually moved to selling and distributing the coddies to other vendors and delis all over town, and Cohen Deli trucks could be seen delivering the popular delicacy all over Baltimore. Considered the poor man's crab cake, they were widely sold at local drugstores and bowling alleys for as little as a nickel throughout Baltimore during the 1960s. The Cohen family continued selling coddies from their own food stands until the 1970s. Considered an iconic Baltimore snack, coddies can still be found at Faidley's Seafood, which has been located in the historic Lexington Market since 1886. Lexington Market, which was established in 1782, is one of the longest-running markets in the United States.

Makes 16 to 24 cakes

1 pound salt cod
1¼ pounds white potatoes
2 tablespoons milk
1 tablespoon unsalted butter
1 small yellow onion, diced
1 tablespoon fresh parsley, finely minced
¼ cup crushed saltine crackers
2 large eggs, lightly beaten
1½ teaspoons Old Bay Seasoning
½ teaspoon freshly ground black pepper

Coddies. *Author's collection.*

French's yellow mustard, for serving
Saltine crackers, for serving

Place the cod in a large bowl and cover with water. Cover with plastic wrap and place in the refrigerator to soak the cod overnight. The following day, check the fish for saltiness. If salinity is at an acceptable level, then simmer cod in water for 8 to 10 minutes; if it's still too salty, add the cod to a pot of water and bring to a boil. Drain immediately, add water to the pot and then simmer the cod over low heat, as above.

Peel and small dice potatoes. Heat a medium saucepan over medium-high heat, adding water and the potatoes and cooking them until fork tender. Using a colander, drain the potatoes and add them to a large bowl. Add the milk, mash the potatoes and set aside to cool.

In a cast-iron skillet, melt the butter. Add the onion and sauté until transparent, about 5 minutes. Remove the skillet from the heat and stir in the parsley.

Using a fork, flake apart the cod well. Remove any bones that may be present. Add the remaining ingredients to a large bowl and combine with the mashed potatoes, onion mixture and crushed crackers. Using a small spoon, form golf ball–size balls and flatten slightly to make a rounded oval.

In a deep cast-iron skillet, add the oil to the depth of 1 inch and heat on high until the oil reaches a temperature of 375 degrees Fahrenheit. Using a Chinese spyder, gently add the cakes into the oil and fry the cakes in batches. Fry on one side until golden brown for 1 minute. Using a spatula, turn the cakes over and fry the other side. The cakes brown quickly, so be sure not to burn them.

Remove the cakes and drain on a paper towel–lined baking sheet. Add more oil to the skillet and bring the oil back to temperature. Repeat the frying process with the remaining cakes.

To serve, add four coddies to a plate with 8 crackers. Serve at room temperature with French's yellow mustard on the side.

Cook's Notes:
To properly eat a coddie, make a sandwich by placing a single coddie on top of a saltine, followed by a dollop of yellow mustard. The sandwich is then topped off with a second saltine cracker.

BAKED TROUT WITH OYSTER STUFFING

The earliest reference for a recipe for oyster stuffing can be traced back to England with the publication of the 1685 cookbook The Accomplisht Cook. *The cookbook describes a number of methods where oysters were being used in stuffing for a variety of meat dishes. By the 1720s, English cooks were stuffing and baking fish, as it was documented in* The Cook's and Confectioner's Dictionary, *published in 1723. In this particular cookbook, one will find a stuffing recipe for fish where eggs, chives, parsley, truffles, mushrooms and an optional mix with bread crumbs were soaked in milk. For a modern twist, you can wow any crowd with this recipe for a whole fish packed with an oyster stuffing that gets citrus hints with the finishing drizzle of a lemon butter sauce.*

Serves 4 to 6

For the trout:
½ stick butter
2 green onions, minced
2 ribs celery, minced
1 large carrot, diced
1 tablespoon chopped fresh parsley
2 teaspoons minced fresh dill weed
1 pint oysters, shucked, drained, coarsely chopped, with liquor reserved
½ tablespoon fresh lemon juice
½ cup light cream
1 teaspoon salt
½ teaspoon cayenne pepper
½ teaspoon freshly ground black pepper
4 cups stale bread cubes
8 8-ounce boneless rainbow trout fillets
2 tablespoons clarified butter
2 teaspoons paprika

For the lemon butter sauce:
1 stick butter
1 cup Chardonnay
1 tablespoon fresh lemon juice
1 tablespoon chopped fresh dill weed or parsley

Preheat the oven to 400 degrees Fahrenheit.

To make the stuffing, in a sauté pan, heat the butter and cook the green onions, celery and carrot for about 2 to 3 minutes. Stir in parsley, dill, oysters and lemon juice and simmer for 1 to 2 minutes. Stir in the cream and season with the salt, cayenne pepper and black pepper. Add the bread cubes, stir and remove from the heat.

Divide the stuffing evenly among the fish, packing it loosely in the fish. Fold the fish to cover the stuffing and place the trout on a buttered baking pan. Brush each trout with the clarified butter. Bake until skin is brown and crisp, about 15 to 20 minutes.

While the fish is baking, make the lemon butter sauce. Cut the stick of butter in half. Reserve ½ the stick of butter, keeping it whole, while dicing the other half into small cubes. Heat a sauté pan over medium heat. Add the ½ stick of butter, allowing it to melt. Gently stir in the wine and lemon juice. Cook until the liquid is reduced by one-third. Whisk in the cubed butter bit by bit until the sauce is silky and smooth. Add the herbs to finish the sauce.

Sprinkle the paprika onto the trout during the last 3 minutes of cooking. Nap with lemon butter sauce just before serving.

VIRGINIA BLUE CRAB PIE

The Virginia blue crab pie may have appeared sometime in the mid-1800s and may have evolved from English savory fish pies, but using seafood that was locally available at the time. This crab pie is a rich, savory, almost quiche-like pie that will make a tasty lunch or brunch dish with a salad or cup of soup. This version is made with crabmeat and Swiss cheese. A small amount of nutmeg and sautéed minced shallots will provide extra flavor.

Serves 6 to 8

For the pastry crust:
2 cups sifted all-purpose flour
1 teaspoon salt
⅔ cup vegetable shortening
5 to 7 tablespoons cold water

For the crab filling:
1 tablespoon butter
2 tablespoons shallots, minced
1 ½ cups lump or backfin blue crabmeat
1 tablespoon flour
1 ½ cups Swiss cheese, shredded and divided
3 eggs
1 cup heavy cream
½ teaspoon salt
Dash white pepper or hot pepper sauce
Dash nutmeg
½ tablespoon chopped fresh parsley

Heat the oven to 425 degrees Fahrenheit and position the rack in the center of the oven.

To make the pie crust:
Sift together the flour and salt. Cut in shortening with a fork until pea-sized pieces are formed. Sprinkle 1 tablespoon water over pastry mixture. Toss with a fork and push to one side of the bowl. Sprinkle with another tablespoon of water. Repeat until all the pastry is moistened. Gather

pastry into a ball and divide the pastry in two. Lightly flour a clean work surface and roll out the pastry ⅛ inch thick.

Line a 9-inch pie plate with the rolled-out dough. Flute the edges and cover the top of the pastry with parchment paper or foil. Fill with pie weights or dried beans at least two-thirds full.

Bake for 10 to 15 minutes, or until just barely pale golden in color. Remove the crust from the oven and carefully remove the paper or foil and weights. Return the crust to the oven for about 5 minutes, or until it is just lightly browned. Remove it from the oven and let it cool.

To make the filling:

In a skillet over medium heat, melt the butter. Sauté the minced shallots until tender, about 2 minutes. Combine the shallots with the crabmeat and flour; set aside.

Sprinkle ¾ cup of cheese in the prepared pie shell, then top with the shallot and crab mixture. Sprinkle with remaining ¾ cup of cheese.

In a bowl beat the eggs, cream, salt, pepper, nutmeg and parsley until well blended. Pour on top of the cheese and crab layers into the pie shell.

Bake for 25 to 30 minutes, or until inserted knife comes out clean (ovens vary).

Remove from the oven and allow to cool before serving.

THOMAS DOWNING

Oysters are often seen as a luxury food now, but throughout much of early American history, they were so abundant that people from all classes regularly ate them. In coastal cities, you could have them on the street or in dingy bars for practically nothing. In late 1800s New York, a man named Thomas Downing (1791–1866) became New York's most famous oyster caterer and businessman who built a potent cultural presence and an empire out of an oyster bar over his forty-year career. But here's the thing: he was a Black man doing this during the era of slavery.

His dignified ethos, active participation in the world of associations, commercial success, forwardness in projecting himself in various public arenas, culinary skill and careful cultivation of print and visual media—all gave rise to a celebrity whose reputation spread beyond Manhattan to the nation in the decade before the Civil War. As a culinarian, he championed professionalism and quality. As a politician, he championed civil rights for African Americans. As a cultural leader, he championed education and social organization. He lived long enough to see the slave system abolished and his sons established in commerce and politics. Upon his death in 1866, newspapers memorialized him as a Gotham landmark, an African American leader and a paragon of self-cultivation and self-discipline. According to the *New York Times* of April 12, 1866, "His death, though at the maturity of life, cannot but excite lively emotions. For industry, patient energy, and heroism, he had few superiors."

A native of Chincoteague on the eastern shore of Virginia, Thomas Downing was born to parents manumitted by a master, Captain John Downing, who had been inspired to free them by the Methodist evangelical teachings about Christian brotherhood. Thomas Downing's parents, who assumed their former owner's rather famous name, had been appointed caretakers of the church's meetinghouse, established by the Downing family in 1783, in Accomack County, Virginia, on the eastern side of the Chesapeake Bay. The church is still standing in Oak Hall, although it was rebuilt after the original structure burned down in 1854. They also managed to acquire land near the inlets around Chincoteague Island, land probably allocated to them by their previous owner. His family and their lifestyle revolved around clamming, digging, raking oysters and fishing. That was his family's everyday livelihood. When Captain Downing died, his heirs attempted to revoke the Downings' liberty, including that of their son Thomas. This attempt at repossession was resisted by force from the African American community, which resulted in the death of one of the white Downing heirs during an attempted seizure. Fleeing for his life, Thomas Downing left Virginia during these troubles and came north, enlisting in the army. He fought in the War of 1812. In 1813, he moved to Philadelphia, where he married and worked as a housepainter. He lived in Philadelphia through 1819.

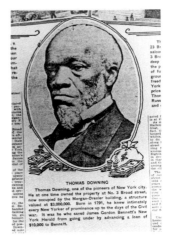

Thomas Downing (1791–1866). *New York City Public Library*.

In 1820, Downing moved to New York; secured a space at 5 Broad Street, near Wall Street; connected with several coastwise traders at the waterfront; and, using connections with oystermen at his old home, began shipping oysters to Manhattan, serving them at his stand in the business district. Oysters, being a seasonal product, required that Downing undertake other business during summers. By the late 1820s, through clever marketing, he informed the city that he had "first rate" oysters for sale, and he began styling his oyster parlor as Downing's Refectory. Downing became a full-fledged restaurateur in 1842 when he opened his Oyster Saloon at 245 Broadway. This three-story building accommodated clubs and private families on its top floor and the general public on its second, and it sold oysters in the shell and jarred pickled oysters retail on the ground floor. He assured the curious that he was "perfectly acquainted with the best method of preparing Pickled, Stewed, Fried or Boiled oysters. He will also provide, in the most modern style boned Turkies, Alamode Beef, Hams, Tongues, jellies, etc." This business would remain in operation until 1857.

As an abolitionist, Downing's concern for the condition of African Americans was profound. He used his Broadway restaurant as a way station of the Underground Railroad. He was a supporter of Frederick Douglass. He belonged to the New York Anti-Slavery Society, the African American branch of the Odd Fellows and the Prince Hall Freemasons and spoke at abolitionist meetings with fire and conviction. His religious beliefs were strong, and he was a member of the only African American congregation in New York, the St. Philip's Episcopal Church, initially called the Free African Church of St. Philip. As a man known for his generosity, he not only supported the church but also donated money to those in need. His authority in the African American community was underwritten by his success as a businessman. He amassed a fortune; owned Manhattan real estate; educated his sons, George W. and Peter, in Europe; and monopolized the high-end oyster trade until the Civil War. His pickled oysters, sold in stoneware jars bearing his name, became ubiquitous. Indeed, New Year's Day in Manhattan was not considered sufficiently celebrated unless Downing's pickled oysters appeared on the table.

He also built up a catering enterprise as well, to which early nineteenth-century events managers turned to provide the food whenever a new steamboat was to be launched, or any big company opened up its doors, or some socialite decided to throw a party or for special governmental occasions. Downing, being "the great man of oysters," was asked to provide the refreshments for the famous Boz Ball that was arranged to welcome English author Charles Dickens in 1842 to the city, when over three thousand New Yorkers turned up in his honor. It was a massive event, impressing the British writer, who was treated like a modern-day rock star. Included in the

The descendants of Thomas Downing. Seated in the *front row, center*, is Downing's son George Thomas Downing (1819–1903), who followed in his father's footsteps, becoming a prominent businessman and a politician who championed civil rights. *New York Public Library*.

WHITE WASHER, water colourer. and house cleaner. – Thos. Downing respectfully informs his customers and the public in general that he removed from the old stand, No. 5 Broad street, near Wall street, to the corner of Nassau & Pine streets, where he will be happy to receive all orders in his line.

☞After the first of May he will be found at his *old established stand* No. 5 Broad, near Wall street, where he will keep his oyster stand also, as usual.   a13 3 w

A re-creation of an 1825 advertisement for Thomas Downing and his whitewashing business, also referencing his "old established stand No. 5 Broad…, where he will keep his oyster stand also, as usual." The year 1825 is the first time Downing appears in the local city directory as an "oysterer" at 5 Broad Street. Based on period advertisements, Downing definitely seems to have been running an oyster stand out of 5 Broad even prior to 1825, when oystering was not his primary occupation. *Author's collection.*

sumptuous feast were fifty thousand oysters, ten thousand sandwiches, forty hams, seventy-six tongues, fifty rounds of beef, fifty jellied turkeys, fifty pairs of chicken, twenty-five pairs of duck and two thousand mutton chops—before the desserts were brought out! Downing was paid $2,200 for his efforts, a princely sum in those days. The party's attendees included the Astors, the Jacobs and the mayor of New York. Dickens later made New York pay for its hospitality, describing the city's most acclaimed food as "piles of indigestible matter," taking special note of the oysters "disappearing down gaping gullets—a solemn and awful sight to see." However, Queen Victoria, another international customer, was a much bigger fan. She was so tickled with the "very choice" oysters Thomas Downing had shipped to her that she sent Downing a gold chronometer watch in gratitude.

When Thomas Downing died in April 1866 at age seventy-five, he died an extremely wealthy man. His death produced an outpouring of grief and nostalgia, for he was one of the most recognizable persons of "Old New York." Downing's wake was reported by the *New York Times* in stirring detail, from the "long line of carriages, well filled with mourners," to multiple delegations of Scottish Rite, York and Prince Hall Freemasons in full regalia. Crowds thronged the streets in front of a church that was packed from its doors to its pulpit, waiting for a chance to view "for the last time the face of him who was well known to all." As a mark of respect, the New York

City Chamber of Commerce closed for the day of his funeral, something it simply doesn't do on a weekday. Its members, among them the most prosperous merchants in Manhattan, had decided they would rather go to Downing's funeral. Downing died the patriarch of a dynasty of politically active and aesthetically refined caterers. The Downing name inspired respect and reverence in New York; Newport, Rhode Island; and Washington, D.C., well into the twentieth century.

OYSTER PAN ROAST

When Thomas Downing opened an oyster restaurant on Broad Street in New York City, he became famous for two things: pickled oysters and his oyster pan roast. This modern adaptation of a classic nineteenth-century dish celebrates the legacy of Thomas Downing. Simple and straightforward, this dish is made with chili sauce, Worcestershire, white wine, shallots and cream. The recipe showcases the story of a man from humble beginnings who became the Oyster King of New York and contributed greatly to the fishing industry, the high-society culture of the East Coast and the African American community during his lifetime.

Serves 2

2 tablespoons unsalted butter, plus more as needed
12 oysters, shucked and liquor reserved
1 tablespoon finely minced shallot
⅓ cup dry white wine
1 tablespoon Worcestershire sauce
2 teaspoons Tabasco sauce
2 tablespoons chili sauce
½ cup heavy cream
Salt, to taste
¼ bunch fresh parsley, chopped
Rustic crusty bread, for serving

In a sauté pan over medium-high heat, melt 1 tablespoon of the butter. Add the oysters and sauté until the oysters begin to plump up on both sides and are halfway cooked, about 2 minutes each side. Pull the oysters out of the pan and set aside.

Using the same pan and adding more butter if needed, sweat the shallot until translucent, about 5 minutes. Add the white wine and stir to deglaze the pan. Simmer to reduce the liquid by half, about 2 minutes.

Add the oyster liquor, Worcestershire sauce, Tabasco, chili sauce and cream. Bring to a simmer and let the sauce reduce by half, about 5 minutes.

Add the oysters to the sauce and remove the pan from the heat (the oysters will finish cooking in the hot sauce). Stir in the remaining 1 tablespoon butter and season with salt as needed.

Ladle the oysters into a shallow bowl. Garnish with parsley.

Serve immediately with bread.

WHATEVER HAPPENED TO TURTLE SOUP?

Since pre-Revolutionary days in America, terrapin was eaten along the Atlantic coast by Native Americans, colonists and slaves alike. Just as lobster was once considered a food eaten by those living in abject poverty and was served only to indentured servants and prisoners, the elite dish of terrapin soup was originally restricted as food for slaves in the Tidewater region. As times change, so did culinary tastes.

By the eighteenth century, turtles were an important food staple in the Atlantic. Large female turtles, or cow turtles, were treasured for their meat. The male, or bull, turtles had little value and were generally used for making soup. As turtle meat used in soup making was bland, it was usually spiced with red pepper. Turtles were easy to transport long distances and were held in pens until sold. The earliest written English recipes for dressing sea turtle were given by Richard Bradley (1732) and ascribed by him to a Barbados lady. He did not mention turtle soup, but this soon became a standard feature of English cookery books. Another recipe appeared in the fourth edition of Hannah Glasse's famous book *The Art of Cookery Made Plain and Easy—By a Lady* (1751). Glasse boasts instructions on how "to dress a turtle the West India way," a recipe that comes right after a "cure for the bite of a mad dog," which involves boiling "scraped tin" filings in good ale. American colonists were not far behind their British cousins in both developing a taste for turtle soup and associating its consumption with refinement.

It appears that Charleston, South Carolina, was the first major North American city that developed a market for the consumption of turtle soup in public dining spaces. Given the city's proximity to West Indian and Floridian sources of sea turtles, this is hardly surprising. In 1784, the Charleston Coffee Shop offered "Turtle Soup every Monday, Wednesday and Friday." Soon, competitors such as Moore's Exchange Coffee-House and Tavern and Browne's Eating-House placed similar notices in local papers. By the 1790s, advertisements regularly appeared in New York, Philadelphia, Baltimore and Boston newspapers offering the public "Real Green Turtle Soup!" that was "of the best quantity," while "gentlemen of the city" were urged to partake in dinners in which turtles would be "dressed in the finest style" before heading to the theater.

During the nineteenth century, the humble diamondback terrapin gradually entered the nation's fine dining scene. The native turtle had long fed residents of the Chesapeake, but by the 1830s, the turtle had become one of the region's most coveted foodstuffs. By the end of the nineteenth century, swanky eateries from New York to California featured turtle soup on their menus. New York City's Delmonico's, considered by many to be the best restaurant in the country, was serving turtle soup to its discerning clientele by at least the mid-1800s.

In 1851, Mississippi's Senator Foote and Louisiana's Senator Downs attended a dinner party at Delmonico's at which they slurped down turtle soup and delivered speeches in favor of the 1850 Compromise. Once a staple for slaves, terrapin was now feeding those who controlled the future of the slave trade.

Demand for terrapin continued to grow and reached its height around the turn of the century. The nation's gourmands believed that any restaurant worth its salt ought to serve turtle soup, and they expected the best to use Chesapeake turtles. The Chesapeake region's "tarpinners," as those who caught and sold terrapin were known, worked hard to satisfy the national appetite. Although terrapins were still relatively plentiful, market prices for the Chesapeake diamondback tripled from 1881 to 1882.

According to Paul Freedman, a food historian at Yale, the great fashion for turtle soup petered out in the mid-twentieth century. Freedman researched old menus from the Philadelphia Club, a fancy gentlemen's club, and discovered that terrapin soup was still being served in the 1950s. Some restaurants even packaged the delicacy in some form or another so that diners could take it home to enjoy it. Freedman believes that the degradation of natural habitats by anthropogenic activities may have contributed to driving the turtles to near extinction. As a result of the Endangered Species Act of 1971, most species were protected from hunting, and turtles became even more difficult to procure for chefs and home cooks alike. A form of turtle soup was still found on the menus at New Orleans's Commander's Palace and at the Oyster House in Philadelphia, but more often than not, it did not contain 100 percent turtle meat but a combination of meats such as offal, veal, stewing beef and alligator that were raised on farms and were not collected from wild populations. Though some

Newspaper advertisement for turtle soup. Baltimore Patriot, *1821*.

restaurants, such as Acadiana in Washington, D.C., still include turtle soup on their menus, the death of the turtle trend, coupled with state and federal restrictions on terrapin harvesting, makes it unlikely that we will see a major rebound in popularity anytime soon in the Chesapeake region. For the most part, Maryland blue crabs will remain a draw for large hungry crowds at the local eating establishments, but terrapin soup appears to be a thing of the past.

Emeline Jones

Born into slavery on the estate of Colonel Benedict William Hall of Eutaw, Maryland, near Baltimore, as a young child, Emeline Jones (circa 1832–1912) was trained to be a house servant. Hall's daughter Elizabeth married Horatio Whitridge and took Jones with her to his house in the Little Gunpowder District of Baltimore. Here, Jones grew into womanhood and perfected her cooking skills, preparing meals for the Whitridge family. By 1860, the Whitridge family had freed Jones, who made her way to New York in 1864, working as a private cook to insurance executive Daniel Fearing at his mansion on the corner of Fifth Avenue and Fifteenth Street. One of the guests at the Fearing mansion was "the prince of good fellows" John Chamberlin (1836–1896), a sportsman, riverboat gambler, hotelier and entrepreneur.

Smitten with her dishes, Chamberlin secured the services of Jones in 1868 and built the Monmouth Raceway and Club House in Long Branch, New Jersey, which was a gambling mecca for the wealthy. Chamberlin later opened grand establishments in New York and at Old Point Comfort in Hampton Roads, Virginia. In 1874, he brought Jones with him from Long Branch to be chef for his Washington Club House. Located in the former enclave of the British delegation in Washington, D.C., this gentlemen's retreat was hailed as "the most elaborate and spacious gaming house and restaurant in the United States" and cost $90,000 ($2 million today). A reporter commenting on the cuisine of the club remarked, "The cook, Emeline Jones, is the well-known colossal quadroon woman who has roasted and stewed so daintily at Long Branch." Chamberlin undertook the management of the Carlton Club in New York and brought Jones with him to supply the cuisines. The Carlton Club became during the later 1870s the nexus of the sporting and political worlds. "No dinner of congressman or senator was considered complete without Emeline's Southern specialties." Presidents Garfield, Arthur and Cleveland devoured her dishes and attempted to secure her services for the White House—to no avail.

Jones's famously delicious Lynnhaven oysters, canvasback duck and terrapin stew being served at Chamberlin's establishments was one reason for the support of the rich and powerfully connected. So was his reputation for running a "square game" in his gambling halls and his ability to make friends with people in power. Chamberlin was known and respected in his long life by more public men than any other man who ever contributed to the creature comforts of a notable person who frequented his gaming clubs and hotels. It appeared that he seemed to know everybody; certainly, everybody seemed to know him. Emeline ran every one of his kitchens, and Chamberlin credited her cooking as the driving force of his success.

Chamberlin paid Jones well and treated her with a deference and affection that earned her loyalty. He permitted her to hire out her services to other entities. During the holiday season in New York, Wall Bakery on Sixth Avenue engaged Jones to make mincemeat pies and rolls. These became famous citywide. By the 1880s, she had settled in Manhattan, where she built up a formidable catering business. Her obituary lists a number of prominent New York chefs who trained under her. Most of Emeline Jones's repertoire of recipes has survived in surprising detail. Her expertise in the Chesapeake style of southern cooking was so preeminent among practitioners in the North that newspaper reporters repeatedly interviewed her during the 1890s and 1900s. Jones was most famous for her terrapin stews.

In the days before emancipation, turtles were so abundant all along the Atlantic coast that they were considered a food for the enslaved. Terrapins favor the brackish water of coastal marshes, so they were easier to capture than sea turtles and thus became a valuable protein source for the Indigenous and enslaved populations in coastal areas. So how did a dish associated with Native Americans and the enslaved become the food of the rich and famous? In the first place, terrapins, as well as snappers and other turtles, were overharvested and went from being abundant to scarce. Among the various turtles, terrapins were the most highly prized. The great French chef Auguste Escoffier declared the terrapin to be the king of the turtles. By the 1890s, the scarcity of these terrapins pushed the price of a bowl of terrapin soup to the equivalent of $135 in current dollars. It should also be noted that preparing a terrapin was both difficult and time-consuming. The turtles had to be kept alive until the moment of preparation. As a result, preparing terrapin dishes was left to the professionals, which meant that only the wealthy could afford to eat them. And that was how Emeline Jones made her mark in the world of New York City haute cuisine.

Many people attempted to secure from Jones her famous recipe for stewed terrapin. Count Canino published a version obtained from the lips of John Chamberlin, but the recipe lacked fundamental details about length of cooking.

Chamberlin's death in 1896 prompted a transformation of Jones's career. One of his sporting circle friends, John Daly, hired her to once again run the kitchen in the Club House at Long Branch during the summer racing season. During the remaining nine months of the year, Jones worked out of her home, catering banquets and parties for the men's clubs and for society women. There she worked until her retirement. During her final protracted illness, the Société Culinaire Philanthropique, New York's famous French chefs' society, paid for her care and support and also for her funeral. She died in 1912, remembered and celebrated by a culinary community that she had nurtured.

MOCK TERRAPIN SOUP

If you are a modern-day college sports fan, then you will know that the diamondback terrapin is famous for being the mascot of the University of Maryland, located in College Park, Maryland. But there was a time when the diamondback was the signature delicacy of Maryland cuisine. The species is native to coastal swamps of the eastern and southern United States, ranging from Cape Sable, Florida, to Massachusetts. Terrapin are unique because they are the only turtle in the United States that can survive in the brackish mixture of salt and fresh water found in the Chesapeake Bay. The terrapin was once referred to as a lowly "trash food" and was served to slaves and prisoners. Terrapin would later rise to the realm of a rare culinary delicacy for the wealthy. Subsequently, soup and the taste for terrapin declined as the animal was overharvested. This follows the usual pattern of boom and bust that "follows the water" of Chesapeake cuisine. Because of the rise of environmental issues, the establishment of the Endangered Species Act of 1971 and sustainably sourced meats and seafood that are available in most local and global markets, many culinary enthusiasts, professional chefs and home cooks alike feel as if there is a stigma against serving turtle. It seems

African Americans catching terrapin with baited poles near Annapolis, Maryland, 1879. *Maryland Historical Society.*

as if true diamondback terrapin soup has drifted into the realm of forgotten culinary history. This is a modern version of mock terrapin soup that uses beef sirloin to mimic the texture of green turtle. Alligator meat can also be used as a suitable substitute.

Serves 6 to 8

2 pounds beef top sirloin, well trimmed
4 cups beef broth
2 cups chicken broth
½ cup unsalted butter
2 medium carrots, chopped
2 large onions, chopped
½ cup minced celery
2 cloves garlic, minced
¼ cup all-purpose flour
1 cup dry red wine
1 bay leaf
½ teaspoon dried marjoram
¼ teaspoon dried thyme
2 whole cloves
¼ cup tomato puree
Salt, to taste
Freshly ground black pepper, to taste
1 dash red pepper sauce
½ cup heavy cream
¼ cup dry sherry
2 tablespoons freshly squeezed lemon juice
2 tablespoons finely grated lemon zest
1 tablespoon Worcestershire sauce
4 hard-cooked eggs, chopped, for garnish
2 tablespoons fresh parsley, for garnish

Chop beef into small cubes, then combine beef and stocks in 6-quart Dutch oven or stockpot. Bring to boil, reduce heat and simmer about 1 hour, skimming foam from surface as it accumulates.

Mock turtle soup. *Author's collection.*

MOCK TERRAPIN SOUP

Meanwhile, heat butter in large cast-iron skillet over medium heat. Add carrots, onion, celery and garlic and sauté until the vegetables are slightly softened, about 5 minutes. Stir in flour and cook 1 or 2 minutes more. Add vegetables and wine to Dutch oven.

Taking a square of cheesecloth, lay the bay leaf, marjoram, thyme and cloves on the cheesecloth and bring all four corners together, making a bag; secure with kitchen twine. Add the bag to the Dutch oven. Stir in the tomato puree. Cover and continue to simmer the soup for about 1 hour, stirring occasionally. Stir in salt, pepper and hot pepper sauce. Simmer for another hour. Blend in the cream, sherry, lemon juice, lemon zest and Worcestershire sauce. Taste and adjust seasoning if necessary. Remove cheesecloth bag and discard.

Serve in bowls and garnish with hard-cooked eggs and parsley.

Brunswick stew. *Author's collection.*

Venison and green corn stew. *Author's collection.*

Left: Ramps. *Brent Hofacker. Adobe Stock Images.*

Below: Fried lobster and skunk bean succotash. This is an original recipe based on ingredients found in the Indigenous and African food pathways. *Author's collection.*

Roasted turkey. *Fahrwasser. Adobe Stock Images.*

Eleanor Parke Custis Lewis (Mrs. Lawrence Lewis) as painted by Gilbert Stuart in 1804.
National Portrait Gallery.

Right: This was long thought to be a portrait of Hercules Posey by Gilbert Stuart but was revealed in 2018 to have been painted by an unknown artist of an unknown man of African descent. *Wikimedia Commons.*

Below: Hoecakes, as enslaved chef Hercules Posey would have prepared for George Washington. *Author's collection.*

Pawpaw pudding. *Author's collection.*

Pawpaw botanical drawing, circa 1801. The pawpaw (*Asimina triloba*) is the largest fruit native to North America and tastes like a combination of a mango, banana and citrus. *Library of Congress.*

Pepper-Pot: A Scene in the Philadelphia Market, as painted by John Lewis Krimmel, 1811.
Philadelphia Museum of Art.

Left: Spiced gingerbread cake with whipped cream. *Author's collection.*

Below: Marinated asparagus with quail eggs, cooked in the manner of James Hemings at Monticello. *Author's collection.*

The kitchen at Monticello. The original Monticello kitchen was built in 1770. In 1784, Jefferson took his enslaved body servant James Hemings with him to Paris with the purpose of having Hemings trained in the preparation of French cuisine. A second kitchen renovation may postdate their return in 1789. The first stew stove was replaced with a new model that may have better matched the state-of-the-art stoves whose use Hemings mastered in Paris. A third kitchen was constructed during the expansion of the main house and was completed by 1809. The newer workspace was much larger and included a bake oven, a fireplace and an eight-opening stew stove with integrated set kettle. A tall case clock also stood in the kitchen. Isaac Granger Jefferson, an enslaved blacksmith at Monticello, later recalled that the only time Jefferson went into the kitchen was to wind the clock. This photograph is the restored kitchen of 1809 that visitors see today when touring Monticello. *Edwin Remsberg. Alamy Images.*

Aerial view of Monticello, showing the house, Mulberry Row and vegetable garden. *Smithsonian Institution.*

Above: Vegetable garden at Monticello. Jefferson, like many plantation owners, used rations as a method to control the enslaved. Although rations were meager at Monticello and at other large estates, the method of rationing food acted as an incentive for slaves to work and comply with the grueling demands of the plantation. The ability to forage for wild resources, raise poultry and grow personal gardens gave the enslaved a measure of control in their lives. *Jill Lang Alamy Images.*

Left: Oeufs à la neige, or snow eggs, are a classic French dessert of small poached meringues floating in a custard sauce. This dessert was prepared by classically trained chef de cuisine James Hemings, who was enslaved by Thomas Jefferson at Monticello. *Author's collection.*

Left: The famous Senate navy bean soup. *Author's collection.*

Below: This deliciously rich pound cake made with butter and orange blossom water was a specialty of Mrs. Elizabeth Goodfellow, a remarkable pastry chef who not only had her own sweet shop and catering business but also ran America's first cooking school for young ladies from elite families in the early 1800s in the city of Philadelphia. *Author's collection.*

R.M.S. "TITANIC."

APRIL 14, 1912.

LUNCHEON.

CONSOMMÉ FERMIER   COCKIE LEEKIE

FILLETS OF BRILL

EGG À L'ARGENTEUIL

CHICKEN À LA MARYLAND

CORNED BEEF, VEGETABLES, DUMPLINGS

FROM THE GRILL.

GRILLED MUTTON CHOPS

MASHED, FRIED & BAKED JACKET POTATOES

CUSTARD PUDDING

APPLE MERINGUE   PASTRY

BUFFET.

SALMON MAYONNAISE   POTTED SHRIMPS

NORWEGIAN ANCHOVIES   SOUSED HERRINGS

PLAIN & SMOKED SARDINES

ROAST BEEF

ROUND OF SPICED BEEF

VEAL & HAM PIE

VIRGINIA & CUMBERLAND HAM

BOLOGNA SAUSAGE   BRAWN

GALANTINE OF CHICKEN

CORNED OX TONGUE

LETTUCE   BEETROOT   TOMATOES

CHEESE.

CHESHIRE, STILTON, GORGONZOLA, EDAM,
CAMEMBERT, ROQUEFORT, ST. IVEL,
CHEDDAR

Iced draught Munich Lager Beer 3d. & 6d. a Tankard.

Above: Chicken Maryland with corn crab fritters. *Author's collection.*

Left: Chicken Maryland was on the menu that was given to the first-class passengers on the day before the sinking of the *Titanic*. *Tim Ireland. Alamy Images.*

Shakshouka. *Sławomir Faje.*
Adobe Stock Images.

Avgolemono (Greek chicken
soup). *Annaileish. Adobe Stock
Images.*

Left: Borscht. *Vankad. Adobe Stock Images.*

Below: Cheesecake. *Nelea Reazanteva. Adobe Stock Images.*

This page: Brodetto is a fish stew and is the signature dish of almost all Italian Adriatic coastal cities, Venetian Lagoon, Romagna, Marche, Abruzzo and Molise. It consists of several types of fish stewed with spices, vegetables and red or white wine. The most important aspect of this dish is its simplicity of preparation and the fact that it is typically prepared in a single pot. It is usually served with polenta or toasted bread, which soaks up the fish broth. *Author's collection.*

Virginia ham biscuits. *Author's collection.*

MORE THAN JUST NAVY BEANS

Is it rude to say that maybe all that hot air coming out of the U.S. Senate is due to loquacious politicians' intake of the famous Senate bean soup? U.S. Senate bean soup, or simply Senate bean soup, is a soup made with navy beans, ham hocks and onion. It is served in the Senate dining room every day, in a tradition that dates back to 1903. The original version included celery, garlic, parsley and possibly mashed potatoes as well.

This ubiquitous dish, like other iconic foods, has an origin myth that's indisputable. According to the myths, two senators, Senator Fred Dubois of Idaho and Senator Knute Nelson of Minnesota, are credited with either requesting the soup or providing the recipe, but their recipes differ slightly. The base recipe includes navy beans, water, smoked ham hocks and onions, but Dubois's version includes mashed potatoes. While this is a satisfying, hearty soup, the only thing that makes it remarkable is that people are still talking about it

John Egerton writes in his book *Southern Food* that the use of ham hocks suggests an origin in southern cuisine. Although the legislators credited with institutionalizing the soup did not represent southern states, most of the cooks in the U.S. Capitol Senate kitchen at the time were Black southern chefs who would prepare bean soup in their own style. There was a period when the Senate dining services omitted the ham and instead used a soup base. In 1984, a newly hired kitchen manager at the U.S. Senate Dining Room discovered this practice; he reflects, "We went back to the ham hocks, and there was a real difference."

The navy bean, haricot, pearl haricot bean, Boston bean, white pea bean or pea bean is a variety of the common bean (*Phaseolus vulgaris*) native to Central and South Americas, where it was first domesticated over ten thousand years ago and traveled to North America with the migration of Paleo-Indian tribes. Most foods that originated in the United States can be traced back to the Indigenous peoples of North America, and the Native American foodways eventually passed on to the European settlers who colonized these lands while bringing indentured servants and later African slaves to these shores. It is difficult to imagine a meal without Native American foods—corn, potatoes, squash and beans. Beans were and still are an integral part of the Native American diet. Often called the "poor man's meat," beans are rich in protein, supplying a third of the essential amino acids to the corn, bean and squash trinity. These native foods were adopted and transformed by enslaved and free Africans and immigrant communities, who added their own traditions, recipes and ingredients to the melting pot.

But is it possible that Senate bean soup has its real origins in western and northern Africa? For example, there is a Moroccan dish called loubia that is made with white beans. Loubia is often served as a side dish or starter to accompany Moroccan cuisine or roasted meats. In the antebellum South, white beans were referred to as soup beans and were sometimes cooked with pork fat. This simple dish became a staple in the diets of the enslaved and poor white, where soup beans were usually served with cornbread, greens and potatoes and may be topped with raw chopped onions or ramps. Soup beans are considered a main course but also serve as a side dish. In rural areas, where food was scarce during the winter, these dried beans still serve as a staple food today.

In these modern times, beans sold as "white beans" in the United States and Canada are usually either navy beans or Great Northern beans. Navy beans, as their name might suggest, were used as a primary food supply by U.S. naval forces in the early 1900s. They are typically the smaller of the two and are popular in soups and stews. They break down easily when exposed to heat, which makes them excellent thickeners. Great Northern beans tend to hold their shape better than navy varieties but often take longer to cook and have a nuttier, denser flavor. The Great Northern is often likened to a miniature lima bean owing to its slightly flattened shape.

No matter what the common bean may be, whether they are black, red kidney, pink, pinto, Great Northern or navy beans, they are a great source of fiber. For the record, navy beans have about nineteen grams of fiber per cup. So, if you don't have a taste for the famous Senate bean soup, you can always add some smoked turkey, kale, onions and carrots for a hearty soup that may suit your taste buds.

THE FAMOUS SENATE RESTAURANT BEAN SOUP

Senate bean soup is on the menu in the U.S. Senate's restaurant every day. Although it is similar to navy bean soup, no one has been able to corroborate its culinary origins. This recipe was adapted from both the 1903 recipe and the current version featured on the daily menu at the U.S. Senate's Dining Room on Capitol Hill in Washington, D.C.

Serves 8

2 pounds dried navy beans
4 quarts hot water
1½ pounds smoked ham hocks
1 large russet potato, peeled and quartered
2 tablespoons unsalted butter
1 onion, chopped
2 stalks celery, chopped
4 cloves garlic, chopped
Kosher salt, to taste
Freshly ground black pepper, to taste
Half a bunch of fresh parsley, chopped, for garnish

Wash the navy beans and run hot water through them until they are slightly whitened. Place beans into pot with hot water. Add ham hocks and simmer approximately 3 hours in a covered pot, stirring occasionally.

While the beans are simmering, bring a medium saucepan of lightly salted water to a boil and add the potato. Reduce the heat and simmer until the potato is fork tender, 20 to 25 minutes. Drain the potato; transfer to a bowl with the milk and mash with a potato masher or fork until smooth. Set aside.

Remove ham hocks and set aside to cool. Dice meat and return to soup.

Heat a large skillet to medium-high and melt the butter; add the onion, celery and garlic and sauté until the vegetables are soft and translucent, 5 to 10 minutes. Remove the skillet from the heat and add the vegetable mixture to the soup. Add the mashed potato to the bean soup and stir until combined. Reduce the heat to low and cook 1 hour, adding up to 1 cup of water if the soup is too thick. Taste and adjust the seasoning with salt and pepper as needed.

Before serving, bring the soup to a boil. Ladle into soup bowls and garnish with parsley and serve immediately.

Chicken Maryland

Unraveling the culinary history of chicken Maryland is like pulling on a loose thread on a fraying sweater that may end up being a ball of yarn to create a brand-new sweater.

The dish goes by a number of aliases in the culinary world, including Maryland fried chicken, chicken Maryland, Maryland chicken and chicken à la Maryland. Some would even say that chicken Maryland is a French rendition of an American recipe. Even minus the "à la," the dish's reversed word order betrays its transatlantic quality.

The first time I ever heard of chicken Maryland was in the novel *Tender Is the Night* by F. Scott Fitzgerald, first published in 1934. Born in 1896 in St. Paul, Minnesota, to an upper-middle-class family, Fitzgerald was named after his famous second cousin three times removed on his father's side, Francis Scott Key, but was always known as plain Scott Fitzgerald. His father was Edward Fitzgerald, of Irish and English ancestry, who had moved to St. Paul from Maryland after the Civil War and was described as a "quiet gentlemanly man with beautiful Southern manners." His mother was Mary "Molly" McQuillan Fitzgerald, the daughter of an Irish immigrant who had made his fortune in the wholesale grocery business. Fitzgerald was the first cousin once removed of Mary Surratt, hanged in 1865 for conspiring to assassinate Abraham Lincoln.

Nicole Diver, the anti-heroine of F. Scott Fitzgerald's final novel, *Tender Is the Night,* is described as "the exact furthermost evolution of a class," in Fitzgerald's words, and in command of the most exquisite manners and taste. She has an excellent ear for foreign languages. However, it is only well into the book that the reader discovers that Nicole is not truly in command of anything. She is a schizophrenic, very much like Fitzgerald's equally glamorous wife, Zelda, mentally unbalanced and hovering constantly on the edge of mania. Throughout the book, she is trying desperately to keep it together, reassuring herself that "everything is all right—if I can finish translating this damn recipe for Chicken à la Maryland into French."

Seventeenth-century descriptions of colonial fare ignored the humble chicken for the most part. In the earliest manuscripts to enter America there are, of course, chicken recipes for roasts, stews and pies, and none other than Governor William Byrd II was dining on the iconic southern dish of fried chicken at his Virginia plantation by 1709.

By the mid-1700s, the efficient and simple cooking process of frying food was very well adapted to the plantation life of African American slaves, who were often allowed to raise their own chickens. The idea of making a sauce or gravy to go with fried chicken must have occurred early on, at least in Maryland, where such a match came to be known as "Maryland fried chicken." Before that, the dish was referred to by many different names. The main distinction of chicken Maryland is that it does not contain the multitude of seasonings and herbs that are found in most fried chicken recipes. The chicken is fried in a shallow pan, most commonly a cast-iron skillet, rather than deep fried in lard or oil like southern fried chicken. The traditional recipe for chicken Maryland is very basic, and it is often suggested to be eaten cold the following day.

During its existence from 1881 through 1971, "the B&O Dining Car and Commissary Department rarely turned a profit, but the railroad believed that if it provided superior dining and impeccable courtesy, it would attract passengers, shippers and investors," according to Greco and Spence's *Dining on the B&O*. Many of the railroad's recipes were originally sourced from Charles Fellows's 1904 book *The Culinary Handbook*. The *Handbook*'s author had a disdain for the affectation of "à la," and thus the recipe is listed here as "Chicken Maryland." Ultimately, the recipe is derived from that book as well as multiple versions of the B&O's culinary references and chefs' notes. Based on the different B&O *General Notice* manuals, the chicken in this dish may have been fried or baked at various times during the height of its existence. I opted to bake it since I've done the whole frying thing before. Rather than gravy, a béchamel sauce that called for a quarter cup of "Mushroom Essence or purée" was to be served over the chicken.

It should also be noted that other versions of this dish were served with some type of banana accompaniment, be it banana fritters or sautéed bananas, mainly because bananas became one of Baltimore's prime imports around the time this dish became popularized in the United States. The dish was also offered on the very last menu of the doomed maiden voyage of the *Titanic* in 1912 and was served only to the first-class passengers.

CHICKEN MARYLAND WITH CORN CRAB FRITTERS

Serves 4 to 6

2 cups buttermilk
1 whole chicken (3 to 4 pounds), cut into 8 serving pieces, backbone reserved
1 cup all-purpose flour
Kosher salt, to taste
Freshly ground black pepper, to taste
4 slices uncooked bacon
Vegetable oil, for frying
2 tablespoons unsalted butter, plus extra for basting
1 ½ cups whole milk

Add the buttermilk and the chicken to a large bowl. Cover with plastic wrap and place the bowl in the refrigerator. Brine the chicken for several hours or overnight for best results.

Remove the chicken from the brine. In a shallow bowl, season flour with salt and pepper. Season chicken lightly with salt and pepper and dredge each piece in flour, shaking off excess. Reserve seasoned flour.

Preheat oven to 400 degrees Fahrenheit.

Heat a cast-iron skillet over medium heat. Fry the bacon until crispy and brown. Place the bacon on paper towels to drain the fat and set aside. Pour off grease into a heatproof container and set aside. Return skillet to burner.

In a large cast-iron skillet, heat ¼ inch oil over high heat to 350 degrees Fahrenheit. Carefully lay chicken pieces in hot oil, skin side down, and fry until lightly browned, 1 to 2 minutes. Using tongs, turn chicken and brown lightly on other side. Turn chicken once more so that it's skin side down again and cover skillet. Cook, covered, for 2 minutes. Remove cover and continue frying chicken, turning as necessary, until well browned on both sides and just cooked through, about 5 minutes longer. Transfer chicken to a wire rack set over a baking sheet and sprinkle lightly with salt. Brush with melted butter. Transfer to oven and bake until internal temperature reaches 180 degrees (about 35 minutes), basting frequently with butter.

Pour off the oil into a heatproof container and return skillet to burner. Add butter and cook until melted and foamy, whisking to scrape up any browned bits. Add 2 tablespoons of reserved seasoned flour, whisking to form a paste. Whisk in milk and cook until a smooth gravy forms that coats the back of a spoon, about 3 minutes. Season gravy with salt and a generous amount of black pepper.

Place the chicken onto serving plates and ladle the gravy on top. Serve with corn and crab fritters, collard greens and mashed potatoes, if desired.

Corn and Crab Fritters
Makes about a dozen 2-inch fritters

1 can sweet corn, well drained
3.7 ounces fresh crabmeat, picked
½ cup grated cheddar cheese
¼ cup fresh basil, chopped
¼ cup fresh parsley, chopped
⅛ cup fresh chives, finely chopped
2 tablespoons all-purpose flour
2 tablespoons yellow cornmeal
Cooked bacon, reserved from above, crumbled
1 large egg
¼ teaspoon black pepper
¼ cup vegetable oil for frying
Finishing salt, such as Fleur de Sel

Add the corn, crab, cheese, basil, parsley, chives, flour, cornmeal, bacon, egg and black pepper into a bowl and stir well to combine.

Prepare a paper towel–lined wire rack.

Heat the vegetable oil in a frying pan over medium heat until shimmering. Add the fritter mixture 1 heaping tablespoon at a time to the pan and fry until golden brown on one side.

Gently flip the fritter over with a spatula and give it a light press to flatten it out, then fry until the other side becomes golden brown and crisp.

Drain the fritters on paper towels, and then sprinkle with finishing salt before serving.

ST. MARY'S COUNTY SOUTHERN MARYLAND STUFFED HAM

Southern Maryland stuffed ham, also known as St. Mary's County stuffed ham, is traditional culinary treasure dating back to the early seventeenth century in the Chesapeake region. Like so many gustatory delicacies, this one was borne of fresh ingredients that were locally available. The exact origins of southern Maryland stuffed hams are unknown, but evidence points to the plantation slaves of the region creating this culinary masterpiece. After butchering the hogs, the plantation owner would keep the finer cuts of pork—ham and bacon, and also sausages—for himself and then give the lesser parts to the slaves. In an effort to extend what little meat these pieces of pig provided, slaves devised a way to make the most of what they were given. Taking the field cress, cabbage, kale and mustard greens that they were allowed to grow in their personal garden plots, slaves took the small pieces of meat provided by their masters and stuffed them along with a heaping handful of spices such as red pepper, mustard seed, salt and black pepper. As was the custom of the day, they boiled everything together in a kettle to infuse the meat with as much flavor as possible. Once the plantation owner tasted the delicious blend of pork and greens made from lesser cuts and realized that the recipe worked well with a more desirable ham, the stuffed ham found its place on the master's dining table. The dish was traditionally prepared in the late winter or early spring, and it was almost always around for Easter holiday celebrations. Southern Maryland stuffed ham is truly one of America's most regionally specific dishes. As an acquired taste, it has never really ventured much beyond St. Mary's County.

This recipe is adapted from a recipe from the St. Mary's County office of the Maryland Cooperative Extension Office, where, for ease of preparation by the modern cook, the stuffed ham may be boiled or baked.

Serves 8 to 12

1 cured ham, 10 to 14 pounds

For the stuffing:
3 pounds kale
3 pounds cabbage
6 to 8 medium onions
6 to 8 stalks celery

For the seasonings:
1 to 3 tablespoons salt
1 tablespoon ground cayenne pepper
1 tablespoon crushed red pepper flakes
1 tablespoon ground black pepper
2 tablespoons celery seed
3 tablespoons mustard seeds

Special equipment:
Cheesecloth
Meat thermometer
30- to 40-quart stockpot
Roasting bag

Keeping the ham in its original wrapper, place it in the refrigerator, where it will remain until it is ready to be stuffed.

To make stuffing, using a chef's knife, finely chop the vegetables. Bring a large stockpot of salted water to boil. Wrap vegetables in cheesecloth and drop in boiling water for several minutes. Remove from boiling water, unwrap cheesecloth and spread vegetables on a sheet pan for rapid cooling.

Once the vegetables have cooled, add them to a large mixing bowl. Add all of the seasonings to the vegetables and mix thoroughly, using a wooden spoon. Cover the bowl with plastic wrap and place stuffing in refrigerator, allowing the flavors to meld overnight.

The next day, remove ham from refrigerator, unwrap and place onto a non-slip, clean cutting surface. Using a chef's knife, cut several rows of deep, vertical slits, about 2 inches apart, down into the ham. Turn ham over and cut perpendicular slits on the other side. Be careful not to let the slits meet. These slits are where the vegetable mixture will be stuffed into the ham.

Place ham in a large container to help minimize the cleanup. Stuff each slit on both sides of the ham with the vegetable mixture. Any leftover stuffing can be placed on top of the ham. Wrap ham in a triple layer of cheesecloth and tie one end in a large knot.

To boil the ham:

Place ham on a rack in a large 30- to 40-quart stockpot and fill with water. Cover and bring to boil. Cook approximately 25 minutes per pound (weight of stuffing and ham combined). Cook until an internal temperature of 165 degrees Fahrenheit is reached. Prepare a rimmed sheet pan by placing a rack on top of it to catch the excess water draining off the ham once it has been removed from the pot. Remove ham from pot and place on rack to drain and cool only long enough so the ham can be handled.

Place ice cubes and cold water in a large roasting pan or clean and sanitized sink. Place ham in a large plastic turkey roasting bag. Leave the bag partly open to "breathe." Place it in the ice water bath to cool quickly. Add additional ice to keep the water cold. Allow the ham to cool in the water (about 2 hours). When completely cooled, place ham in refrigerator for at least 6 hours, or overnight for best results.

When ready to serve, remove the ham from the bag. To serve, slice the ham across the grain so each slice contains stuffing and meat. Slice thinly for sandwiches or thick for entrée portions, adding a bit of stuffing on the side as a condiment.

To bake a stuffed ham:

Heat oven to 325 degrees Fahrenheit and bake at 15 minutes per pound for hams weighing more than 12 pounds; bake at 18 minutes per pound for hams weighing less than 12 pounds; or at 22 minutes per pound for half of a ham.

When the ham is done, remove to the oven and place on a wire rack to rest and cool for 15 to 20 minutes. Once the ham has cooled, slice and place the slices on a serving platter and serve.

CHAPTER 6

The Immigrant Experience

THE EUROPEAN IMMIGRANT EXPERIENCE

Beginning in the in the mid-1600s, port cities like Jamestown, Philadelphia and Baltimore served as an early entryway for immigrants entering colonial America and settling along the East Coast. And over time, for the most part, New York Harbor eventually served as the gateway for all of Europe to enter the Mid-Atlantic region during the rise and fall of Ellis Island between 1892 and 1954. Even in the present day, JFK Airport in Queens, New York, serves as the modern port for many immigrants seeking a better life in the land that is known as America. But looking into the past, it should be noted that the regionalism of colonial America could be defined by its political, economic and religious factions. For example, the Tidewater part of the southern colonies represented the typical English gentleman, modified by a warm climate. By the eighteenth and nineteenth centuries, slave labor and living in an aristocratic baronial fashion on great plantations were firmly established in the Carolinas and Georgia. On the other hand, in the cool climates of the Northeast, New England stood for frugality and the establishment of English Puritanism.

But the Mid-Atlantic colonies were less English than all the other regions. This area had a wide mixture of nationalities, a varied society, a mixed town and county system of local government and a thriving economy. It should be noted that the Mid-Atlantic also varied in many religious sects. After being expelled from Spain and South America, Jews made a home first in New York and subsequently Philadelphia, despite the colonial government's reluctance to host them. Catholics attempted to establish Maryland as their only safe haven in English North America. And as time passed, formerly enslaved men and women founded churches of their own in Pennsylvania, which had long served as a refuge for those wanting to practice religion as they pleased. In short, it was a region mediating between New England and the South and the East and the West. The Mid-Atlantic actually represented that composite nationality that would come to be defined in the contemporary United States as "American" in terms of identity and culture, with the juxtaposition of non-English groups occupying a valley or a little settlement and presenting reflections of the map of immigrants from a variety of European countries. Some historians would believe that the Mid-Atlantic region was democratic and nonsectional, if not national; "easy, tolerant, and contented"; and rooted strongly in material prosperity. In comparison to other North American colonies, the Mid-Atlantic was least sectional, not only because it lay geographically between North and South but also because with no physical barriers to shut out its frontiers from its settled region, and with a system of interconnecting waterways, the Mid-Atlantic region mediated between East and West as well as between North and South with relative ease and thrived. Thus, the Mid-Atlantic became the typical American region.

Within this context, the immigrants coming to America brought their own cultures and food traditions with them to the New World. And by the same token, so many of the so-called American foods that originated in their homelands and were re-created with whatever ingredients were available in their locale were passed on from the Indigenous people to early European settlers and literally became the cornerstone of modern-day American cuisine. Before and after the American Revolutionary War, these "American foods" were adopted and transformed by immigrant communities, who added their own traditions, recipes and ingredients to the melting pot. And as circumstances allowed, immigrants brought their food preferences and eating customs with them as the North American colonies transitioned into the United States, allowing them to maintain a sense of identity and cohesion.

In terms of the mid- to late nineteenth-century immigration, one of the most dominant immigrant groups that flooded into the Mid-Atlantic pre–Civil War was the Irish refugees fleeing food shortages almost beyond modern comprehension. As early as the fall of 1845, the *Baltimore Sun* reported the "most dreadful of calamities" under the headline "FAMINE IN IRELAND." In a country of 8.5 million, more than 1 million people would die of starvation and famine-related diseases because of potato crop failures and indifferent British policies. Another 1.5 million Irish fled to America. More than a few of these desperate immigrants arrived at Ellis Island in New York City and on the banks of Fells Point—the original point of entry into the city of Baltimore—near death, according to contemporaneous accounts. Others did not survive the month-long journey aboard what became known as "coffin ships." Those who did survive were employed doing the backbreaking, dangerous work of digging tunnels and building bridges or toiling in warehouses. Underscoring their low socioeconomic standing, Irish workers often labored alongside enslaved and free African Americans.

During the same time, the failed 1848–49 German revolution—the country was then a collection of confederate states—combined with feudalism, conscription, oppression and their own potato famine convinced hundreds of thousands of Germans that immigrating to the new democracy of the United States was worth risking the harrowing transatlantic journey. The enclaves of New York City and Baltimore also became a haven for Jewish Germans fleeing anti-Semitic laws. The newcomers tended to cluster in the poorer districts of the metropolises. Most of them settled in the great commercial, industrial and cultural centers of New York and then Philadelphia, Boston, Baltimore and the Midwest, in particular Chicago. Certain neighborhoods in these cities became almost exclusively Jewish, congested and bustling with a rich, typically Jewish way of life. The number of European Jews living in Baltimore rose from 120 in 1820 to an estimated 7,000 by the onset of the American Civil War.

Immigration then came to a near standstill during the Civil War. The arrival of the first foreign steamship—appropriately named the *Baltimore*—at the new immigration piers at Locust Point was greeted on March 23, 1868, with a cannon salute as it passed Fort McHenry and a parade down Broadway. These German travelers were following in the footsteps of earlier German immigrants to Baltimore. Over the next five decades, the steady flow of Norddeutscher Lloyd ships from the ports of Bremen, Germany, would rechart the city's course and character. By the 1880s, Poles, Lithuanians, Slovaks, Bohemians, Russians, Ukrainians and Eastern European Jews boarded the North German Lloyd line ships for Locust Point. Like the earlier German immigrants, the new immigrants from Eastern Europe were pushed by economic hardship, fear of conscription, class discrimination and, in the case of Jewish people, continued pogroms in Europe. Meanwhile, steamships, replacing sailing vessels, made the North Atlantic trek smoother and safer.

"New York—Welcome to the land of freedom—An ocean steamer passing the Statue of Liberty." Scene on the steerage deck from a sketch by a staff artist appearing in *Frank Leslie's Illustrated Newspaper*, July 2, 1887. *Library of Congress.*

From the opening of the Locust Point piers in 1868 until they closed in 1914—the period between the end of the Civil War and the start of World War I—1.2 million European immigrants entered Baltimore's Ellis Island, making the city the third-busiest port of entry in the United States and the busiest below the Mason-Dixon line. The influx of immigrants built the city's ethnic neighborhoods around the harbor, and the foods and cultural customs they brought with them, just like the immigrants before them, changed the foods of the Mid-Atlantic. Germans introduced crunchy molasses-based gingerbread and sugar cookies in Pennsylvania, and the Dutch introduced cinnamon-based cookies, all of which have become part of the traditional Christmas meal. Did you know that scrapple was originally a type of savory pudding that early Pennsylvania Germans made to preserve the offal of a pig slaughter? The Philadelphia soft pretzel was originally brought at the beginning of the eighteenth century to eastern Pennsylvania, and later, nineteenth-century immigrants sold them to the masses from pushcarts to make them the city's best-known bread product, having evolved into its own unique recipe. Philadelphia pepper pot, a tripe stew that was originally an African dish transported to the Caribbean and later adopted by the British, is considered a classic of home cooking in Pennsylvania alongside bookbinder soup, a type of turtle soup.

And for the record, New York–style hot dogs came about with German-speaking immigrants from Austria and Germany, particularly in the case of the frankfurter sausage and the smaller wiener sausage. Today, the New York–style hot dog with sauerkraut, mustard and the optional cucumber pickle relish is such a part of the local fabric that it is one of the favorite

Mohamed Juda from Algeria poses for a photo outside Ellis Island's main building. Photo by Augustus F. Sherman, 1910. *New York City Public Library*.

comestibles of New York City. Hot dogs are a typical street food sold year round in all but the most inclement weather from thousands of pushcarts. As with all other stadiums in Major League Baseball, they are an essential for New York Yankees and New York Mets games, though it is the local style of preparation that predominates without exception. Hot dogs are also the focus of a televised eating contest on the Fourth of July in Coney Island, at Nathan's Famous, one of the earliest hot dog stands opened in the United States in 1916.

During the early twentieth century, other dishes found in the Mid-Atlantic came about that have much to do with delicatessen fare. Delicatessens were set up largely by Jewish immigrants from Eastern Europe who came to America incredibly poor and most often unable to partake in the outdoor food markets that the general population utilized. The influence of European Jewry on modern Mid-Atlantic cooking remains extremely strong and is reinforced by their many descendants in the region. American-style pickles, brought by Polish Jews, are now a common addition to hamburgers and sandwiches, and Hungarian Jews brought a recipe for almond horns that now is a common regional cookie that diverts from the original recipe in dipping the ends in dark chocolate. New York–style cheesecake has copious amounts of cream and eggs because animal rennet is not kosher and thus could not be sold to a large number of the deli's clientele. New York inherited its bagels and bialys from Jews, along with challah, the bread today most favored for making French toast in New York, New Jersey and eastern Pennsylvania. Pastrami first entered the country via Romanian Jews and is a feature of many sandwiches, often eaten on marble rye, a bread that was born in the Mid-Atlantic. Whitefish salad, lox and matzah ball soup are now standard fare made to order at local diners and delicatessens but started their life as foods that made up a strict dietary kosher code.

Italians and Greeks also came to the Mid-Atlantic, establishing communities that became known as Little Italy or Greektown. They generally came by train, often from New York, because there was no direct steamship service from the south Mediterranean region to Baltimore.

Within years of settling into their adopted countries, each immigrant group made sure the ingredients they loved and craved were available for consumption or suitable substitutions were made. For example, in the Italian American communities of the late nineteenth century, in the backyards of their adopted cities, gardens were established and fennel and tomatoes were grown, while their Thai counterparts who arrived in the late 1960s grew fresh cilantro and mint.

THE GREAT MIGRATION

It is also important to keep in mind that the story of European immigration is not meant to serve as a complete history of the development of the food pathways found in the Mid-Atlantic nor the identity of the region as a whole. The Great Migration—the broad movement of African Americans leaving the Jim Crow South for the North—took place, for the most part, after the largest waves of immigration along the Eastern Seaboard to cities like Baltimore, Harlem and Philadelphia, sometime between 1910 and 1970. It's worth noting that Blacks fleeing the South left for many of the same push/pull reasons immigrants did—economic opportunity, full citizenship, freedom from persecution and hopes of a better education for their children. Others were running for their lives, seeking to dodge the renewed outbreak of lynchings and violence encouraged during the Woodrow Wilson administration. And with them, they, too, brought their own culinary tradition and also encountered food traditions of the European immigrants.

Within the context of the Great Migration, the environment resulted in the incorporation of new food pathways and the development of new dishes within African American food traditions. Much of this transfer, passing along and creating new dishes happened in the African American restaurants, diners and soul food places that developed to serve these new

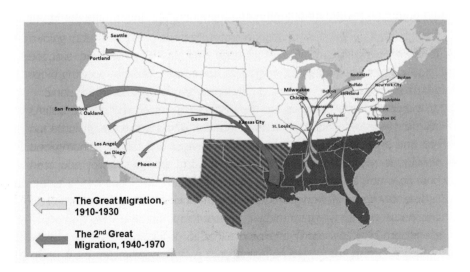

The Great Migration. *Author's collection.*

The Arthur family arrived at Chicago's Polk Street Depot on August 30, 1920, during the Great Migration. Scott and Violet Arthur arrive with their family in Illinois at Chicago's Polk Street Depot, two months after their two sons, Herman Arthur (1892–1920) and Irving Arthur (circa 1901–1920), were lynched in Paris, Texas, by a white mob on July 6, 1920. This picture was published by the *Chicago Defender* on September 4, 1920, and it has become an iconic symbol of the Great Migration. Chicago Defender/*Chicago History Museum*.

urban communities of African Americans from the South. Black consumers began to incorporate various foods into their food traditions. Some of these foods included the use of Polish sausage in gumbos and stews, sauerkraut borrowed from the German culture and served with baked ham and oven-baked spaghetti with bread and tossed salad, borrowed from the Italian American communities. In this sense, one might compare the experience of African American migrants in the North and the Mid-Atlantic to the experiences of foreign immigrant groups across our collective history, from the Germans, Irish, Scandinavians, Chinese, Italians, Mexicans, Koreans and Vietnamese to the Somalians, Ethiopians and other more recent arrivals from Latin American countries and the Middle East.

THE IMMIGRANTS OF LATIN AMERICA

In the twenty-first century, many of the current wave of immigrants are from Mexico and Central America. They, too, have encountered circumstances in establishing their communities in a new world that would have been familiar to the earlier Baltimore immigrants of 150 years ago. They confront similar language and cultural barriers, stereotypes and discrimination, low wages—exploitation by employers and politicians—and backlash from entrenched, previous immigrant ethnic groups.

Unlike many other immigrants, Latin American immigrants were able to retain most of their food culture with access to ingredients grown in Central America. Mexican groceries were fairly common in areas of the United States that had large populations of Latin Americans. The cuisine of Central America—in particular Mexico, Guatemala, Honduras, El Salvador, Nicaragua and Costa Rica—is drawn from the Indigenous culture and is a fusion with European cooking. And like in the Mid-Atlantic, these dishes utilize corn, beans, beef and seafood in creating some of the best food in Central America. Once again, the Mid-Atlantic region was introduced to a whole new world of cooking with meat, spices and root vegetables. Latin American cooking relies heavily on spicy peppers and chilies, along with meat. Another example of common Central American food is the introduction of the tortilla, which can be eaten plain, with meat or filled with cheese. The salsa we eat today is another example of the many different kinds of spicy sauces used in traditional Central American cooking. Beans, prepared mashed and fried, were introduced to American culture as well, transforming the food pathways in the Mid-Atlantic.

For the most part, homegrown ingredients remain very much at the heart of Mid-Atlantic cuisine, as shown by the vast popularity of the farmers' markets and community-supported agricultural co-ops found in urban cities and rural towns everywhere. Supermarkets have also responded to the needs of their consumers, as store shelves are stocked with a range of ethnic foods that have become so much a part of the American palate.

SHAKSHOUKA

Historians have traditionally identified Jewish immigration to the New World with three specific eras: Sephardic, German and Eastern European. Each group had an impact on the American Jewish community and, subsequently, the cuisine of the Mid-Atlantic. Food has played an important role in Jewish American communities since the first Sephardic Jews, who trace their history from Spain and Portugal, arrived in New Amsterdam from Brazil in 1654. New Amsterdam was a Dutch colony that settled on what is now the southern tip of Manhattan Island of New York. During the colonial era, Jews adapted their cooking to the foods grown regionally in their new surroundings. They learned to use corn, beans and fish, such as salmon, herring and cod, while also continuing to observe the Jewish dietary laws, or Kashrut. By 1655, they had established a presence in southwestern Pennsylvania long before King Charles II deeded the land to William Penn in 1682. Penn embarked on his "holy experiment," creating a colony where anyone who lived peacefully was welcomed, and established the city of Philadelphia. Within time, Philadelphia not only became the city of brotherly love but also became the city of almonds, pomegranates, olive oil, chickpeas, lentils, dates, grapes and fava beans, all thanks to the Jews who introduced colonial America to these Mediterranean foods connected to centuries-old Jewish culture.

Today, Sephardic cuisine refers to the foods eaten by a large and diverse group of Jews from Spain, Morocco, Tunisia, Algeria, Libya, the Middle East, Egypt and Turkey. A popular Sephardic dish known as shakshouka involves eggs poached in a spicy tomato sauce. Tunisian Jews are credited with bringing shakshouka to Israel. The dish has slowly caught on in the United States and is considered a simple vegetarian meal that can be served for breakfast, lunch or dinner. This recipe is a modern variation of a traditional shakshouka with the addition of feta cheese, which softens into creamy nuggets in the oven's heat.

Serves 6

3 tablespoons extra-virgin olive oil
1 large onion, halved and thinly sliced
1 large red bell pepper, seeded and thinly sliced
1 small habanero pepper, seeded and finely chopped

A Jewish merchant, a Somalian Jewish woman and other Yemenite Jews, Aden, Yemen, historical engraving, 1886. *Alamy Images.*

1 small jalapeño pepper, seeded and finely chopped
2 Thai red bird chilies, finely chopped
3 garlic cloves, thinly sliced
1 teaspoon ground cumin
1 teaspoon sweet paprika
⅛ teaspoon cayenne, or to taste
1 28-ounce can whole plum tomatoes with juices, coarsely chopped
Salt, to taste
Freshly ground black pepper, to taste
1 teaspoon tomato paste
Pinch of brown sugar, optional
5 ounces feta cheese, crumbled
6 large eggs
Fresh chopped cilantro, for garnish

Preheat the oven to 375 degrees Fahrenheit.

Heat oil in a large cast-iron skillet over medium-low heat. Add onion, bell pepper and chili peppers. Cook gently until vegetables are very soft, about 20 minutes. Add garlic and cook until tender, 1 to 2 minutes; stir in cumin, paprika and cayenne and cook 1 minute.

Pour in tomatoes and season with salt and pepper; add tomato paste and brown sugar, if using, and simmer until tomatoes have thickened, about 10 minutes. Stir in crumbled feta.

Using a wooden spoon, make several wells in the simmering tomato sauce. Gently crack eggs into skillet over the tomato wells. Sprinkle with salt and pepper. Transfer skillet to oven and bake until eggs are just set, 7 to 10 minutes.

Garnish with cilantro and serve with pita or a rustic bread.

STUFFED GRAPEVINE LEAVES

A significant number of Greeks did not begin immigrating to the United States until the 1880s. Between 1900 and 1920, more than 350,000 Greeks immigrated to the United States, and 95 percent of them were men. Upon arrival, most Greek immigrants found jobs in various industries, textile mills, copper and coal mines and working on railroad gangs. In keeping with Greek tradition, these men often worked to secure dowries for their sisters back home. They often lived in boardinghouses with other Greek men, eating communal meals of familiar foods involving grains, spiced meats and fresh vegetables cooked in olive oil.

The Greeks introduced America to dishes like spanakopita, a phyllo pastry pie of spinach and feta cheese filling; stuffed grapevine leaves (dolmas); and gyros served with tzatziki sauce. After the first decade of the twentieth century, the pattern of Greek immigration came to include entire families intent on remaining in the United States. Greek immigrants began going into business for themselves, opening shoeshine parlors, candy shops and, most notably, restaurants. Their first restaurants served native cuisine to fellow Greeks and later to the general public. Using mainly family members for labor and requiring little startup money, the restaurant business was the first stable economic base for Greeks in America. By 1919, one out of every three restaurants—most of them being diners in the Mid-Atlantic—was operated by a Greek family.

This Greek appetizer is perfect for vegetarians, as it is made from tender grapevine leaves wrapped into little rolls and stuffed with rice, tomatoes and fresh herbs. Dolmades are traditionally served in Greek households as part of a meze platter and are a staple on the menus at the numerous Greek-owned diners in the Mid-Atlantic.

Makes 24 rolls

2 large yellow onions, finely chopped
½ cup olive oil
1 head garlic
1 tomato, chopped
1 cup lemon juice
1 tablespoon tomato paste
Kosher salt, to taste
Freshly ground black pepper, to taste

STUFFED GRAPEVINE LEAVES

1 cup cooked white rice
¼ cup chopped dill
1 16-ounce jar of commercially prepared grape leaves
Lemon wedges, for serving

Place the onions and oil in a skillet and cook over medium heat until the onions are soft and translucent, about 10 minutes. While the onions cook, peel the garlic cloves and mash them to a paste in a mortar and pestle. Add this to the pan along with the tomato, lemon juice, tomato paste and salt and pepper to taste. Cook for another 5 minutes. Stir in the rice. Remove the pan from the heat and stir in the dill. Set aside to cool to room temperature, then refrigerate for at least 1 hour.

While the filling is cooling, drain the grape leaves and carefully pull them apart. Remove the stems and place them into a large bowl and cover them with cold water. Let them soak until you are ready to roll.

Heat the oven to 350 degrees Fahrenheit.

Place a grape leaf on your work surface, shiny side down. Add 1 tablespoon of the rice mixture to the middle of the grape leaf. Fold the sides over the rice and roll the leaf into a small log shape, about the size of your thumb. Repeat with the remaining rice filling, placing the stuffed leaves into a 9x9-inch baking dish. When the dish is full, cover the stuffed leaves with several layers of flat grape leaves and pour in 1 cup of water. Cover and bake for 1 hour. Remove from the oven and let cool to room temperature and refrigerate.

Serve this appetizer cold or at room temperature with a squeeze of lemon.

CHICKEN SOUP WITH EGG-LEMON SAUCE (AVGOLEMONO)

Avgolemono is one of the best-known Greek soups, made with egg yolk and lemon juice mixed with broth and heated until they thicken. My godfather, George Tartarus, came from a large Greek family. He and his wife, Lily, did not have any children of their own, but during school vacations, we spent a lot of time in the kitchen with George, and he taught my brother and me how to cook some of his favorite dishes. He learned these recipes from his mother and grandmother and passed them on to us. His favorite soup was avgolemono, which can be considered the equivalent of the classic American chicken noodle. Although avgolemono is a mealtime staple throughout the year, it holds a place of honor at the table during Easter dinner, as well as being a taste of memories for me. The second-largest influx of Greeks came in the 1950s—coinciding with the heyday of Greek diners. Avgolemono became a staple on the menus at Greek diners during that era and entered the modern food pathway of Mid-Atlantic cuisine.

Serves 8

1 3- to 3½-pound whole chicken
12 cups cold water
3 tablespoons kosher salt
1 leek, cleaned and quartered
1 carrot, peeled and quartered
2 bay leaves
3 tablespoons extra-virgin olive oil
1 medium white onion, finely diced
⅔ cup arborio rice
½ cup fresh lemon juice
2 large eggs
1 teaspoon ground white pepper

In a 6- to 8-quart stockpot, combine the chicken, water and 2 tablespoons salt. Bring to a boil over medium-high heat; immediately reduce the heat to a very low simmer. Using a spoon, skim the foam from the surface. Add the leek, carrot and bay leaves and continue to simmer with the chicken until the chicken is thoroughly cooked, about 45 minutes to 1 hour.

CHICKEN SOUP WITH EGG-LEMON SAUCE (AVGOLEMONO)

Meanwhile, heat the oil in a large skillet over medium-high heat. Add the onion and cook, stirring, until translucent, about 6 minutes. Remove from the heat and set aside.

Remove chicken from the broth and allow meat to cool. Strain the broth and skim off any residual fat. When the chicken is cool enough to handle, pull the meat from the bones and discard the skin. Dice the meat into large cubes; refrigerate until ready to use.

Return the broth to high heat, add the rice and onion and bring to a rolling boil. Reduce the heat and simmer until the rice is almost cooked through, about 20 minutes. Add the chicken and reduce the broth to a low simmer.

In a medium-sized bowl, beat the lemon juice, eggs and pepper. Ladle 2 cups of hot broth into a measuring cup with a pourable spout. While whisking, slowly pour the 2 cups of broth into the egg mixture. Pour the egg mixture back into the pot with the remaining 1 tablespoon of salt. Stir well to blend.

Ladle the soup into serving bowls and serve immediately.

BORSCHT

The second wave of Jewish immigration occurred between 1830 and 1880, as they came mostly from Germany, mainly due to religious persecution, restrictive laws, economic hardship and the failure of reform movements that advocated political revolutions. For the most part, German Jews looked to America as an antidote to these ills—a place of economic and social opportunity. And in search of that freedom, they brought with them their food traditions. Their foodways drew upon German national traditions, as well as Jewish religious tenets. Because of the strict dietary laws (Kashruth), no pork was eaten. Most often, they were completely unable to partake in the outdoor food markets that the general population utilized, as most of the food for sale was not kosher. Jewish immigrants settled where religiously sanctioned kosher foods were available. Thus, Jewish marketplaces became the culinary and cultural centers of Jewish communities, offering fruits and vegetables, fish and the meat of animals slaughtered according to religious law. The food was generally simple and hearty and developed as a result of being frugal as well as poor. Famous Jewish foods that came out of this tradition include chicken soup, matzah balls, latkes, gefilte fish, cholent (beef and barley stew), kneidlach (dumplings) and borscht (beet soup).

Borscht is a traditional soup that is common to many Eastern European and Northern Asian cuisines. Beetroot is one of the main ingredients, which gives the soup its distinctive ruby red color.

Serves 8 to 10

For the stock:
3 quarts cold water
1 ½ pounds beef short ribs or oxtails
½ white onion, quartered
2 celery stalks, halved
1 medium carrot, halved
2 bay leaves
5 whole black peppercorns
1 teaspoon salt

For the borscht:
2½ cups medium beets, peeled and grated
3 medium potatoes, peeled and cut into 2- inch chunks
3 tablespoons tomato paste
Salt, to taste
1 bay leaf
2 medium carrots, grated
½ cup medium onion, finely chopped
2 cloves garlic, minced
½ small head red cabbage, cored and thinly sliced
Juice of 1 lemon or 1 teaspoon white vinegar
Freshly ground black pepper, to taste

Sour cream, for garnish
Fresh dill sprigs, for garnish

For the stock:
In a large stock pot, combine water, beef short ribs, onion, celery, carrot, bay leaves and peppercorns and a pinch of salt. Bring to a boil and then reduce the heat to simmer for 1 to 2 hours, until the meat is falling off the bones. Remove any scum that floats to the top with a slotted spoon several times through the process.

Remove the stock from the stove and allow to cool. Remove meat and bones, placing on a separate plate to cool. Using a sieve, strain the stock and discard the vegetables.

When the meat is cool enough to handle, remove it from the bones and shred with two forks. Set aside. Discard the bones.

Return the strained stock to the stock pot.

For the borscht:
Add the shredded meat, grated beets, potatoes, tomato paste, a pinch of salt and bay leaf to the stock pot. Bring to a boil, then reduce the heat to a simmer. Cook for about 20 minutes.

Heat oil in a large skillet over medium heat. Add the grated carrots and chopped onions; sauté over low heat for 5 to 10 minutes until onions have caramelized. Stir in the garlic and fry for less than 30 seconds.

Add the sautéed vegetable mixture to the stock, along with sliced cabbage, and cook for 15 minutes or until the cabbage leaves are tender. Remove the bay leaf. Finish the soup with juice of 1 lemon or 1 teaspoon of white vinegar. Taste and adjust the seasoning with salt and pepper, as needed.

To serve, ladle the borscht into a shallow soup bowl and top with a dollop of sour cream. Garnish with fresh dill, if desired.

LIBERIAN-STYLE COLLARD GREENS

This dish may have originated in Bong, a county in the north-central portion of the West African nation of Liberia. Since 1973, Bong has been a sister city to Baltimore City, but the association of Liberia to the United States is a long one. Beginning in the mid-1800s, there was a movement to resettle free-born African Americans and former slaves who faced racial discrimination in the form of political disenfranchisement and the denial of civil, religious and social privileges in the United States. Most whites and a small cadre of Black nationalists believed that Blacks would face better chances for freedom and prosperity in Africa than in the United States. The American Colonization Society (ACS), a private organization, was founded in 1816 in Washington, D.C. Slaveholders wanted to get free people of color out of the South, where they were thought to threaten the stability of the economy being supported by slave labor. In 1822, ACS began sending Black volunteers to the Pepper Coast to establish a colony for free-born African Americans and the formerly enslaved. The African American settlers carried their adopted southern antebellum culture and traditions with them to Liberia, as well as reconnecting with ancient foods pathways of West Africa. Much of the culture and foods from Liberia are adapted from African American culture.

I first had this dish at a restaurant and was completely blown away by the flavors presented in it. This dish is more like a fish stew with vegetables. At first glance, one may think the ingredients for this dish are a bit strange, but they come together perfectly. Collard greens have long been a staple in African American cooking. My grandmother taught me that when cooking, one has to use all of their senses. According to her, when cooking something like greens, there is no such thing as accurate measurements; you have to feel it, eyeball it, smell it and taste it to get the best-tasting greens. With this dish, you have to adjust the seasonings to your liking, for it can be very spicy. The longer it cooks, the more the flavors will meld, giving an exotic and delightful taste to the palate.

Serves 4 to 6

Liberian greens. *Author's collection.*

6 slices bacon
2 bunches collard greens
⅓ cup vegetable oil
2 cloves garlic, minced
1 cup chicken broth
4 cups water, plus more as needed
3 cubes chicken bouillon
2 smoked turkey wings
⅓ cup creamy peanut butter
Seasoning salt, or to taste
¼ teaspoon crushed red pepper flakes, or to taste
1 teaspoon sugar
Kosher salt, to taste
Freshly ground black pepper, to taste
Two 6-ounce fillets flounder (see Cook's Note)

Arrange a rack in the lower third of the oven and heat to 400 degrees Fahrenheit. Line 1 to 2 rimmed baking sheets with aluminum foil. Lay the bacon on the baking sheet in a single layer and do not overlap.

Bake until the bacon is deep golden-brown and crispy, 15 to 20 minutes, depending on the thickness of the bacon and how crispy you like it. Begin checking around 12 minutes to monitor how quickly the bacon is cooking. When done, remove the bacon from the oven and pour off the residual bacon fat into a heat-proof container. Using tongs, transfer the bacon to a plate lined with paper towels. When the bacon is cool enough to handle, gently crumble and set aside.

Inspect the greens and discard any damaged and chlorotic (yellow) spotted leaves. Wash the greens thoroughly, removing any sand and grit. Drain and, using a chef's knife, remove the tough center stem. Neatly stack several leaves on top of each other and roll them into a bundle that resembles a fat cigar; cut the bundles into thin strips. Repeat this process until all the greens have been cut.

Heat a large stockpot over medium-high heat. Add the oil and garlic and sauté the garlic until slightly golden. Add the chicken broth, water, chicken bouillon, greens and turkey wings. Continue to simmer until greens are wilted, about 10 minutes. Stir bacon, peanut butter, seasoning salt, crushed red pepper, sugar, salt and black pepper into pot. Cover and simmer until greens are very tender and peanut butter begins to separate, about 2½ hours. Add more water if the vegetable mixture becomes too dry.

Using a ladle, remove the turkey wings from the pot to a cutting board. Remove the skin and bones and discard. Shred the turkey meat and return the turkey meat to the pot.

Add the flounder fillets into the simmering greens. Continue to cook until fish breaks down, about 30 minutes more, stirring frequently.

To serve family style, ladle the greens into a large bowl and serve immediately.

Cook's Note:
Catfish, haddock, halibut or any other firm white fish are suitable substitutes for flounder in this dish.

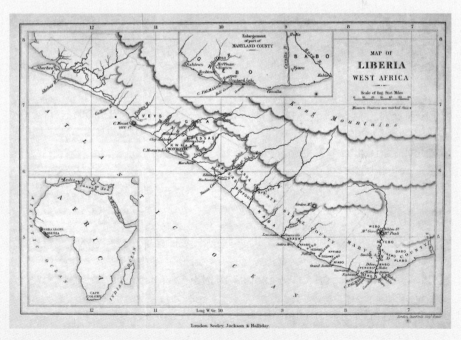

Map of Liberia, West Africa, 1869. *Princeton Theological Seminary.*

OYSTER STEW

The first wave of Irish immigration occurred during the colonial period between 1700 and 1775. Most of the immigrants were Presbyterians and assimilated relatively quickly. When the second wave of Irish immigrants entered America in the eighteenth century, prior to the onset of the Great Irish Potato Famine of 1845–52, many brought with them their culinary traditions of eating fish and shellfish. The vast majority of these Irish immigrants were Roman Catholic, and like the Jews before them, they faced prejudice for their faith. They settled in the cities of Philadelphia, New York and Baltimore, and these cities were not always set up or accommodating for their needs. Like most Catholics of today, they followed strict religious dietary customs around holidays, one of which was to abstain from eating meat on Christmas Eve. In Ireland, the Christmas Eve meal revolved around a fish called the ling, and home cooks made a simple stew using dried ling, milk, butter and black pepper However, Irish cooks could not find dried ling in America and, out of necessity, adapted to using oysters. Today, many families enjoy serving a satisfying dish of oyster stew as part of their Christmas Eve tradition, though it can be enjoyed any time of the year. The most important factors in preparing oyster stew are not allowing the milk to boil and not overcooking the oysters, which causes them to become tough.

Serves 6 to 8

3 dozen fresh oysters, shucked, with liquor reserved
7 tablespoons unsalted butter
1 medium onion, finely diced
1 celery stalk, chopped
Kosher salt, to taste
1 tablespoon all-purpose flour
2 quarts whole milk, warmed
2 cups heavy cream
Pinch cayenne pepper
Freshly ground black pepper, to taste
¼ bunch fresh chives, snipped, for garnish
Oyster crackers, for serving

Oyster stew. *Author's collection.*

Drain the oysters using a very fine strainer to remove and reserve the liquor. Set aside.

In 6-quart Dutch oven, melt about 5 tablespoons of butter over medium-high heat. Reduce the heat and add the onion, celery and salt. Cook slowly, until onions are translucent and the celery is softened, 2 to 3 minutes. Sprinkle in the flour, stirring well to blend, cooking for 2 minutes.

Whisk in the milk, heavy cream and reserved oyster liquor. Add the cayenne pepper. Reduce the heat to a light simmer, stirring often to prevent scorching, for 3 minutes. Remove from the heat and set aside.

Heat a large cast-iron skillet over medium heat. Melt the remaining butter. Add the oysters in a single layer, being careful not to crowd them. Sprinkle a little salt and pepper and sauté until the edges of the oysters begin to curl, slightly revealing the gills.

Add the oysters to the Dutch oven and return to a gentle simmer to warm the stew through. Taste the stew and adjust the seasoning with salt and pepper.

To serve, ladle the stew into shallow soup bowls. Garnish with chives and serve with oyster crackers.

BRODETTO

This fisherman stew was inspired by the local cuisine found in (or near, if more appropriate) the coastal city of Ancona, Italy. This rustic dish simmers the seafood in a garlicky tomato sauce and is served with a crusty bread. Many Italian coastal towns have their own version of this dish, which often features the catch of the day. Brodetto was originally conceived by fishermen to use up the smaller fish that they did not sell at the market that day. While brodetto is similar to the classic French fish stew bouillabaisse, traditional Italian recipes call for thirteen fish, as an acknowledgement of the biblical reference to Jesus and his twelve apostles in attendance at the Last Supper, when it is served for Easter dinner. The stew made its arrival in the Mid-Atlantic region with the massive migration of Italians during the late nineteenth century. The stew can be made with any type of fish; shellfish, including mussels and clams; and either octopus or squid. The key to making this particular recipe is to cook the shellfish and fish in stages. If you are shopping at your local markets and cannot find the listed seafood in this recipe, always choose sustainable varieties that are in season.

Serves 6

6 1-inch-thick ciabatta bread slices
¼ cup extra-virgin olive oil, plus more for brushing and drizzling
5 garlic cloves, divided
1 cup finely chopped onion
½ cup dry white wine
1 32-ounce jar tomato sauce
2 tablespoons white wine vinegar
1 pound mussels, scrubbed
12 littleneck clams, scrubbed
12 ounces cod fillets, cut into 2-inch pieces
12 ounces skin-on snapper fillets, cut into 2-inch pieces
10 ounces raw large shrimp, peeled and deveined
2 teaspoons kosher salt
6 ounces cleaned squid, bodies cut into ½ inch-thick rings
3 tablespoons chopped fresh parsley

Brodetto.
Author's
collection.

Preheat broiler to high with oven rack 4 inches from heat. Brush bread with olive oil and place on a baking sheet. Broil until golden brown, 3 to 4 minutes, flipping halfway through. Rub toast with 1 garlic clove and keep warm.

Thinly slice remaining 4 garlic cloves. Heat ¼ cup oil over moderately high heat in a large Dutch oven. Add onion and sliced garlic; cook, stirring occasionally, until translucent, about 5 minutes. Add wine; boil until reduced by half, about 2 minutes. Add tomato sauce and vinegar; bring to a simmer. Add mussels and clams; cover and cook until mussels open, about 5 minutes. Remove mussels with a slotted spoon and place in a large bowl. (Discard any shellfish that do not open.) Cover pot and cook until clams open, 3 to 4 minutes. Remove clams with a slotted spoon and place in bowl with mussels.

Season cod, snapper and shrimp with salt. Add to pot, cover and reduce heat to moderate; simmer 6 minutes. Add squid, cover and cook until fish are just cooked through, about 2 minutes. Stir in parsley, mussels and clams. Remove from heat. Cover and let stand until shellfish are heated through, about 2 minutes. Serve in shallow bowls with a drizzle of olive oil and garlic toast.

BARBECUED BEEF BRISKET

Traditionally, in Jewish households in the Mid-Atlantic, and in particular in Baltimore, brisket was not a typical food that was served for everyday meals. It was normally served as a main course dish for Jewish holidays, such as Rosh Hashanah and Passover. Brisket is also the most popular cut for corned beef, which can be further spiced and smoked to make pastrami.

Brisket is a large cut of fatty meat from the front of the cow and one of the toughest cuts. As an inexpensive cut of meat, it requires a long cooking time and special preparations to make it tender and flavorful. In traditional Jewish cooking, it is most often braised like a pot roast for several hours. This recipe allows for the low and slow roasting of beef brisket in the oven, which yields a meat that will be so tender that it will practically fall apart. The best part about this recipe is that the leftover brisket can be used in sandwiches, tacos or even a breakfast hash or used in this cookbook's version of Brunswick stew (see page 33).

Serves 6 to 8

For the brisket:
1 3- to 5-pound brisket, fat trimmed to about ¼ inch thick
Kosher salt, to taste
Freshly ground black pepper, to taste

For the brisket rub:
1 packed tablespoon brown sugar
2 teaspoons smoked paprika
2 teaspoons ground cumin
1 teaspoon mustard powder
1 teaspoon onion powder
1 teaspoon garlic powder

For the barbecue sauce:
1 teaspoon vegetable oil
1 large white onion, finely chopped
3 cloves garlic, minced
⅓ cup packed dark brown sugar
½ cup ketchup

1 tablespoon Worcestershire sauce
½ cup apple cider vinegar
¼ cup bourbon
Reserved brisket juices, skimmed of fat

Preheat the oven to 275 degrees Fahrenheit. Place an oven rack in the middle of the oven.

Season the brisket with salt and black pepper.

Prepare the brisket rub in a small bowl; mix all of the spice rub ingredients together until well combined. Gently rub the spice mix all over the brisket.

Using-heavy duty aluminum foil, make a double-layered foil pouch for the brisket: place two layers of foil on the counter, place the brisket (with the fat side up) on the foil and pull the edges of the foil up around the brisket to wrap it. The pouch must be sealed well so that the brisket will remain moist while cooking. Place the prepared brisket in the refrigerator, allowing the spice rub to meld into the meat, for 3 to 24 hours for best results. Note: After using the rub, the brisket can be cooked immediately, if desired.

Place the foil pouch on a baking sheet or in a Pyrex baking dish. Cook the brisket for 3 to 5 hours, depending on the size of the brisket. The internal temperature should be between 180 and 210 degrees Fahrenheit. The meat is at its most tender between 180 and 190 degrees.

Turn off the oven and allow the brisket to rest inside the oven until it's cool enough to touch.

Pour the accumulated juices from the brisket into a large measuring cup and set aside to cool. Skim the layer of fat that has accumulated on top of the juices, saving 2 tablespoons of the fat for the sauce, and discard the rest. Reserve the juices. Meanwhile, keep the brisket wrapped in foil and return it to the warm oven while the barbecue sauce is being made.

To make the sauce, heat the oil in a medium-sized pot over medium heat. Add the onion and cook until softened, 4 to 5 minutes. Add the garlic and cook until fragrant, about 1 minute. Add the brown sugar, ketchup, Worcestershire sauce, apple cider vinegar and bourbon and whisk to combine. Reduce to a simmer and cook for 2 to 3 minutes, until all of the ingredients are blended. Add the reserved brisket juices and continue to simmer until it has reduced to the desired consistency, about 15 minutes.

Remove the brisket from the oven and carefully open the foil pouch, as some steam will be released. Turn the oven to broil. Brush the brisket with a good layer of sauce and broil, uncovered, until the top is lightly browned and the fat begins to crisp. Remove from the oven and allow the brisket to rest before slicing.

To serve family style, slice the brisket against the grain into ¼-inch slices and place on a large platter. Serve with extra barbecue sauce on the side.

CORNED BEEF AND CABBAGE

Corned beef and cabbage is the quintessential St. Patrick's Day meal served in the United States, even if you are not Irish. But ironically, corned beef and cabbage is truly an American dish with British, Irish and Jewish origins. The dish may have been based on the traditional Irish fare of bacon and cabbage. The unpopularity of corned beef in Ireland comes from its relationship with beef in general long before the Roman occupation in ancient times. From early on, cattle in Ireland were not used for their meat but for their strength in the fields, for their milk and for the dairy products they produced. In ancient Gaelic Ireland, cows were a symbol of wealth and were considered sacred animals. Because of their divine association, they were slaughtered for their meat only if the cows were too old to work, produce offspring or milk. The Irish diet stayed pretty much the same for centuries until England conquered most of the country in 1601, marking the collapse of the Gaelic chiefdom system and the beginning of Ireland's history as part of the British Empire.

The British changed the Irish concept of the sacred cow into a commodity, increased beef production and introduced a New World crop, the potato. England outsourced beef production to Ireland, Scotland and eventually North America to satisfy the growing palate of the English people. The British coined the term "corned beef" in the seventeenth century to describe the fact that the salt crystals used to cure the meat were similar to the size of corn kernels. By the end of the eighteenth century, the demand for Irish corned beef began to decline as the North American colonies began producing their own cattle. In 1845, a potato blight broke out in Ireland, completely destroying the potato crops and decimating the Irish population, which led to the Great Famine. Without assistance from the British government, the Irish people were forced to work to death, starve or immigrate to North America and South America.

The second wave of Irish immigration was largely Catholic, and like the Jewish immigrants before them, Irish Catholics were faced with the challenges of prejudice and religious intolerance. Although still poor, they were earning better wages in America and had more money than they had in Ireland under British rule, which brings us back to corned beef. Irish immigrants were able to purchase beef from kosher butchers. What we think of today as Irish corned beef is actually Jewish corned beef tossed into a pot with cabbage and potatoes. In the Jewish community, corned beef was made from brisket, a kosher cut of meat from the front of the cow. The Irish

Corned beef. *Brent Hofacker. Adobe Stock Images.*

Americans transformed St. Patrick's Day from a religious feast day to a celebration of their heritage. It didn't take long for corned beef and cabbage to become a staple in American households. Maybe it was on Lincoln's mind when he chose the menu for his first inaugural luncheon on March 4, 1861, which was corned beef, cabbage and potatoes.

Serves 4 to 6

For the corned beef:
3 pounds beef brisket, trimmed
1 cinnamon stick, broken into several pieces
1 teaspoon mustard seeds
1 teaspoon black peppercorns
8 whole cloves
8 whole allspice berries
2 bay leaves, crumbled
½ teaspoon ground ginger
Fresh ground black pepper, to taste
3 cloves garlic, smashed
1 small onion, quartered
1 large carrot, coarsely chopped
1 stalk celery, coarsely chopped

For the cabbage:
1 large head of cabbage, sliced into ⅜-inch to ½-inch-wide slices

Place the brisket in 6- to 8-quart Dutch oven. Cover the beef with an inch of water. Add all of the ingredients to the pot and bring to a boil; reduce heat to a simmer. Simmer for 2½ to 3 hours, until the beef is fork tender. Remove from pot to a cutting board and allow to rest before slicing. Reserve cooking liquid for boiling cabbage.

Once the corned beef has been removed from the pot, strain the braising liquid and return it to the pot. Add the cabbage to the pot. Taste the braising liquid. If it is too salty, add more water. Raise the heat until the liquid is simmering well. Simmer until the cabbage is cooked through, 15 to 30 minutes.

Place the cabbage in a serving bowl. Add a little of the cooking liquid.

Thinly slice the corned beef against the grain, place on a platter and serve.

FRIED CATFISH

Fried catfish is more of a southern tradition, brought to the Mid-Atlantic during the Great Migration of African Americans to the northern and western United States between 1890 and 1970. They were fleeing the racial oppression of Jim Crow, seeking better social and economic opportunities, and they brought new food pathways with them. Many new transplants began to adapt their diets to the foods that were readily available, including the staples of yellow cornmeal and the abundance of seafood in the Chesapeake Bay. Today, most catfish is farm raised and is readily available in local markets. Whether pan fried or deep fried, it always tastes great with coleslaw, hushpuppies and fries.

Serves 4 to 6

3 to 4 pounds catfish fillets or 8 whole dressed catfish

For the marinade:
½ teaspoon salt
⅛ teaspoon lemon pepper seasoning
Pinch of achiote powder
Juice of 1 lemon

For the seasoned cornmeal:
½ teaspoon salt
1 tablespoon ground black pepper
1 teaspoon cayenne pepper
1 teaspoon garlic powder
1 teaspoon onion powder
2 cups yellow cornmeal
Vegetable oil for frying

Rinse fillets under cold running water and pat dry with paper towels. Set aside. In a shallow baking dish, add spices and lemon juice. Cover with plastic wrap and marinate fillets in the refrigerator for 20 to 25 minutes.

Fried catfish. *Author's collection.*

Combine the cornmeal and spices in a shallow dish. Heat the oil to medium in a large cast-iron skillet. Remove fish from the refrigerator. Shake off excess marinade and dredge fillets in seasoned cornmeal. Fry in the hot oil until golden brown, about 3 minutes. Drain on paper towels and serve immediately with hushpuppies, tartar sauce and coleslaw.

TRENTON TOMATO PIE

The origin story for Trenton tomato pie is a familiar one. Neapolitan immigrants settled in Trenton, New Jersey, finding work in the city's factories. Among these immigrants was Joe Silvestro, who opened a restaurant called Joe's Tomato Pies on South Clinton Avenue in 1910. Silvestro's establishment baked pies—not pizza—in coal-fired ovens. The distinction between pizza and Trenton tomato pies is in the process of making the pie. Old New York pizzerias like Totonno's, Sam's Restaurant and John's on Bleecker Street in Greenwich Village apply tomatoes on top of cheese and call their creations pizza. Unlike the thicker square Italian tomato pie, Trenton tomato pie is often circular, of the crunchy yet thin-crust variety. In this style of tomato pie, the mozzarella and toppings are placed on top of the prepared dough first, followed by lightly crushed tomatoes or tomato sauce placed on top. From a culinary perspective, there's no difference between a tomato pie and a pizza, but Trenton natives will defend their regional style as a singular entity unto itself.

For the record, a December 6, 1903 article in the New York Tribune *uses the phrase "tomato pie" to describe the Italian pomodoro pizza, a thinly stretched dough topped only with tomato. Calling it a "pie" gave unfamiliar patrons, both American and Italian, an easy explanation of the mostly unfamiliar food that was centuries old from the Old World. New Yorkers still cling to the word "pie," using it as shorthand for all types of pizza, but Trenton held onto "pie" as the preferred nomenclature for its particular variation of the dish.*

One of Joe's employees, Joe Papa, learned the trade of making tomato pies at Joe's Tomato Pies and opened his own restaurant, called Papa's Tomato Pies, just down the street two years later in 1912. Although Papa's has moved several times over the past century, it has operated continuously since it first opened, making it the oldest continuously run tomato pie restaurant in the United States. Papa's may be the oldest, but the most famous name in Trenton tomato pie is DeLorenzo's. Pasquale and Maria DeLorenzo emigrated from the town of San Fele, Italy, just east of Naples, and their four oldest sons opened the family restaurant in the late 1930s.

After eighty-nine years in business, Joe's Tomato Pies closed its doors in 1999, leaving Papa's and DeLorenzo's the only remaining tomato pie

Trenton tomato pie. *Author's collection.*

restaurants from the old guard. Although they are still in business, both have closed their Trenton locations and moved to suburbia.

The recipe here is a very simple tomato pie that is baked to be "extra crispy," just like the DeLorenzo's version found in Trenton, New Jersey.

TRENTON TOMATO PIE

Makes one 14-inch pie

1 28-ounce can whole peeled San Marzano tomatoes
¾ teaspoon kosher salt
8 ounces prepared pizza dough, room temperature
All-purpose flour, for dusting the surface
1½ cups mozzarella, shredded, divided
¾ teaspoon extra-virgin olive oil
Crushed red pepper flakes, for serving, optional

Special equipment:
Pizza stone or 2 stackable rimmed baking sheets
Parchment paper

Place a rack in the lowest position of the oven. Set pizza stone or 2 stacked, inverted baking sheets on rack; preheat oven to 500 degrees Fahrenheit for at least 1 hour.

Drain tomatoes in a colander. Crush into small pieces with your hands, drain again and transfer to a medium bowl. Stir in salt; set aside.

Lightly dust a rolling pin with flour and roll out dough to a 14-inch circle on lightly floured parchment paper, making sure dough is evenly thin from center to edge; if dough pulls back when rolling, cover with plastic wrap and wait 5 minutes.

Transfer parchment with dough to a pizza peel, large cutting board or inverted baking sheet. Sprinkle with 1¼ cups cheese. Top with tomatoes. Sprinkle with remaining ¼ cup cheese.

Carefully slide parchment with pizza onto hot baking stone. Bake pizza until crust is deep golden brown, 10 to 12 minutes.

Transfer pizza to a cutting board and let cool 2 minutes.

To serve, drizzle with oil and cut into wedges. Sprinkle with crushed red pepper flakes, if using.

PEPPERONI ROLLS

If you ever have an opportunity to visit southern Italy, chances are that you will not find a pepperoni roll anywhere in the region. The pepperoni roll is a uniquely Italian American food innovation whose origin can be traced back to north-central West Virginia when Italian immigrants came to work in the coal mines.

There were several cultural forces that gave birth to the pepperoni roll, mainly due to need. West Virginians recognize the pepperoni roll as a vestige of the state's coal mining industry. People have worked as coal miners for centuries, but they became increasingly important during the Industrial Revolution, when coal was burned on a large scale to fuel stationary and locomotive engines and heat buildings. Coal miners were among the first groups of industrial workers to collectively organize in protection of both working and social conditions in their communities.

After the late nineteenth century, coal miners in many countries were a frequent presence in industrial disputes with both the management and government. The United Mine Workers of America (UMWA), a labor union, was founded in 1890 and engaged in bitter, though often successful, disputes with coal mine operators for safe working conditions, fair pay and other worker benefits. An industrial union, the UMWA includes miners in bituminous and anthracite coal mines, as well as workers outside the mining industry. After a successful coal miners' strike in 1897, John Mitchell became president (1898–1908) and led the union through a period of rapid growth—despite determined opposition by mine operators.

Since the nineteenth century, coal mines have been locally owned in the United States. The social system revolved not so much around occupation but ethnicity, since nearly all inhabitants were blue-collar workers with similar backgrounds. Welsh and English miners had the highest prestige and the best jobs, followed by the Irish. By the early twentieth century, at a lower status of the coal miner hierarchy stood recent immigrants from Italy and Eastern Europe; recent arrivals from the Appalachian hills were lower status. The ethnic groups would stick together, seldom mingling. African Americans were sometimes brought in as strike breakers. There was little machinery apart from the railroad. Before mechanization began, the miners relied on brute force, pickaxe, hand drills and dynamite to smash lumps of coal out of the walls and shovel them into mule-drawn carts that hauled it to the weighing station and the railroad cars. The culture was heavily masculine, with strength, virility and physical courage held in high regard.

In 1900, West Virginia was home to more native-born citizens than any other state. Before mechanization reduced the need for manual labor, the coal industry boomed and labor needs surged. There was strong anti-union sentiment against the American labor movement and the UMWA. Coal companies sought, as one historian put it, "a more docile, controllable work force than their American-born counterparts." Coal mining companies began to recruit Italian immigrants from Calabria, Italy, to do the dangerous underground extraction work. However, the mining company executives did not get what they bargained for. As it turned out, Italian immigrants were just as inclined, if not more so, toward union affiliation and action. By 1915, there were more Italian laborers than any immigrant or ethnic group working the coal fields and mines of West Virginia.

Italian foods were gaining popularity in West Virginia and the surrounding Appalachian areas in the early twentieth century. With the lucrative mine and railroad operations centered there, many immigrants from Italy were attracted to the region and brought their cuisine with them, eventually sharing it with the local American populace. Out of that cauldron of labor strife and self-determination came a hybridized food that owed as much to West Virginia as it did to Calabria, the region from which so many of the Italian immigrants came. One of these foods was pepperoni rolls, which are elegantly simple but uniquely West Virginian: country roll dough filled with sticks or slices of pepperoni.

Miners would work long hours, and they needed a filling, simple lunch they could take with them into the mines. They would eat comfort foods to sustain themselves while working. The pepperoni roll is similar to the Italian calzone. But given its smaller size and utility, the pepperoni roll is comparable to a number of handheld foods designed for on-the-job consumption by miners. For example, meat-and-potato-stuffed pasties, popular on the Upper Peninsula of Michigan, where copper mining was once important, have their likely origins in the tin mines of Cornwall, England. And it should be noted that the British sausage roll was invented in the mining communities of the United Kingdom to serve the same purpose of portability.

Pepperoni rolls. *Piotr Krzeslak. Adobe Stock Images.*

Pepperoni rolls were first commercially produced around 1927 when a baker by the name of Giuseppe "Joseph" Argiro emigrated from Calabria, Italy, to work in a Clarksburg-area coal mine. Instead, he pooled his resources and opened a bakery in Fairmont, West Virginia. Argiro originally invented the pepperoni roll as a lunch for the local coal miners. He remembered his coal miner friends would sit and eat a stick of salami in one hand and a piece of bread in the other, which can be cumbersome if you are trying to eat in a hurry during a lunch break. So Argiro had an idea: he combined the two ingredients and created the pepperoni roll, a portable, shelf-stable snack that allowed miners to eat with one hand, drink water with the other and then return back to work quickly. In addition to their portability, pepperoni rolls also made an excellent meal for coal miners because they had protein and fat for energy and staving off hunger, and they did not require refrigeration, which made them easy to tuck into a pack or pail and take to the mines on their own with no other preparation needed for them. The pepperoni roll was a success among Argiro's hungry miner customers from the time he invented them. He sold them by the dozen at the bakery for about forty-five cents each.

Other bakeries followed Argiro's example. Tomaro's Bakery, the oldest Italian bakery in the state and just a few miles away in Clarksburg, developed its version of the pepperoni roll around the same time. A handful of other bakers also followed suit. By the 1950s, pepperoni rolls had begun to gain a more generalized popularity among the working class throughout the state, which helped secure the pepperoni roll in West Virginia's food culture.

In 1987, when the United States Department of Agriculture proposed restrictions that threatened to put the family-owned bakeries of pepperoni rolls out of business, West Virginia pepperoni roll producers contacted Senator Jay Rockefeller, who intervened and successfully saved the entire industry.

Argiro's original bakery, Country Club Bakery, is still in operation today, baking up its staple pepperoni roll using the original recipe, made fresh every day.

In the northern reaches of West Virginia, along a corridor of Appalachia stretching from Buckhannon through Clarksburg up to Morgantown, an appetite for pepperoni rolls cuts across class strata and demographics as the food continues to be a beloved regional favorite. If you have a chance to visit West Virginia, you will see pepperoni rolls in stores and gas stations in every city and town. It is a quintessential Appalachian cuisine.

Serves 4

For the dough:
2½ cups all-purpose flour
1 tablespoon kosher salt
1 teaspoon instant yeast
1 cup water

For the pepperoni roll:
¼ cup olive oil, plus more for the baking sheet
1½ pounds sliced pepperoni
½ pound mozzarella cheese
½ pound provolone cheese
2 ounces Parmesan, grated

Marinara sauce, for serving

For the dough:
Combine the flour, salt and yeast in the bowl of a stand mixer fitted with a dough hook attachment. Stir to combine, then add 1 cup water. Mix on low speed until the dough comes together into a rough ball. Continue mixing at medium-low speed until the dough forms a smooth, silky ball, about 10 minutes. Form the dough into a tight ball, set in the bottom of the mixer bowl, cover tightly with plastic wrap and set aside in a warm place until the dough has roughly doubled in size, about 1 hour.

For the pepperoni roll:
Preheat the oven to 375 degrees Fahrenheit. Lightly oil a rimmed baking sheet.

Roll the dough out into a rectangle ¼ inch thick. If the dough isn't stretching well, cover and let rest at room temperature for 30 minutes, then stretch again.

Leaving a ½-inch border, cover the dough with the sliced pepperoni. Cover the pepperoni with the mozzarella, followed by another layer of pepperoni covered with the provolone. Fold over the outside edges of the dough and roll up lengthwise like a jelly roll.

Transfer the roll to the baking sheet, seam-side down. Make 6 shallow cuts on an angle on the top of the roll. Brush the rolls with the remaining oil and sprinkle with the Parmesan. Bake until golden, 25 to 30 minutes.

Serve warm or cold, along with marinara sauce for dipping, if desired.

AMISH POTATO SALAD

Amish potato salad. *Author's collection.*

The history of food exchange and foreign influence in a country is one that often follows trade routes, exploration and colonization. The history of the potato and the development of potato salad in the United States is no exception. It all begins in the sixteenth century, when Spanish explorers discovered the potato, a New World food, in South America and brought the vegetable back to their homeland. From there, the potato was introduced by farmers and merchants to Europe, where it became a food staple.

The earliest known mention of potato salad has been traced back to the sixteenth century in Germany. As a country that developed hundreds of recipes for potatoes, Germany almost certainly was among the first to look at cooked small new potatoes or cut chunks of larger spuds and imagine them blanketed with vinegar-based dressing. The dressing used may have been Roman in origin, which is akin to the heated dressing used to wilt spinach salad. More than likely, with most Germans being familiar with the vinegar bite of sauerkraut and sauerbraten, the common potato was a perfect match. Classic German potato salad evolved from featuring a little coarse mustard to other recipes using sugar to cut the sour taste of vinegar. Some recipe variations will have the addition of bacon (speck) for added flavor. By the late nineteenth century, potato salad was introduced to America by Dutch and German settlers.

This hearty Amish potato salad is known for its distinct egg-enriched, creamy cooked dressing and the sweet-and-sour flavor that comes from vinegar and sugar. This rich dressing is then tossed with hot cooked, cubed potatoes that soak up more of the rich and tangy egg flavor.

Serves 6 to 8

6 medium white potatoes with skin
2 eggs, beaten
¾ cup white sugar
1 teaspoon cornstarch

½ teaspoon salt
⅓ cup apple cider vinegar
½ cup milk
1 teaspoon prepared yellow mustard
3 tablespoons butter
1 cup mayonnaise
1 small onion, finely chopped
1 cup chopped celery
1 cup small dice carrots
1 teaspoon celery seeds
4 hard-cooked eggs, peeled and roughly chopped

To prepare the potatoes, take a very sharp knife and score the potato entirely around the center. Place the potatoes into a large pot and fill with enough water to cover. Bring to a boil and cook for about 20 minutes, or until the potatoes can easily be pierced with a fork.

Remove potatoes and place into a bowl filled with water and ice. Let potatoes sit in the ice water for just a few minutes, until they are cool enough to touch. Holding the potato in both palms on either end, with thumbs pull away the skin from the center, removing all from the potato in 2 pieces. Repeat for all potatoes.

Dice the potato into medium-sized cubes. Cover and set aside.

While the potatoes are cooking, make the dressing. Whisk together 2 eggs, sugar, cornstarch and salt in a saucepan. Stir in the vinegar, milk and mustard. Cook over medium heat, stirring frequently, until thickened, about 10 minutes. Remove from heat and stir in the butter. Cover with plastic wrap and place in the refrigerator for 20 minutes or until cool. Stir in the mayonnaise.

Place the potatoes in a large mixing bowl and toss with the onion, celery, carrots, celery seed and hard-cooked eggs. Gently fold in the dressing.

Using plastic wrap, cover the bowl and refrigerate the potato salad until ready to serve. For best results, allow the potato salad to chill for 24 hours in the refrigerator, allowing the flavors to meld completely.

COLCANNON

Before the introduction of the potato to Irish cuisine, milk, cheese, meat, cereals and certain vegetables composed the Irish diet. After the early eighteenth century, no meal was considered complete without potatoes.

Colcannon is a traditional Irish dish that is composed of a mixture of creamy mashed potatoes and a green vegetable, usually kale or white cabbage, with milk or cream, butter, salt and pepper added. There are also many regional variations of the dish that make use of other ingredients, such as scallions (spring onions), leeks, onions and chives. It is often eaten with boiled ham or Irish bacon.

In Ireland, colcannon is usually eaten in autumn and winter, when kale comes into season during Samhain, a Gaelic New Year festival with pagan origins that is celebrated on October 31–November 1. Samhain marks the end of the harvest season and the beginning of winter or the "darker half" of the year.

Colcannon. *Adobe Stock Images.*

Serves 4

> *4 russet potatoes, peeled and cut into large chunks*
> *Kosher salt, to taste*
> *5 to 6 tablespoons unsalted butter*
> *3 lightly packed cups of chopped kale, cabbage, chard or other leafy green*
> *vegetable*
> *3 green onions, minced*
> *I cup cream*

Put the potatoes in a medium pot and cover with cold water by at least an inch. Add 2 tablespoons of salt and bring to a boil. Boil until the potatoes are fork tender, about 15 to 20 minutes. Drain in a colander.

Return the pot to the stove and set over medium-high heat. Melt the butter in the pot, and once it's hot, add the greens. Cook the greens for 3 to 4 minutes, or until they are wilted and have given off some of their water. Add the green onions and cook 1 minute more.

Pour in the cream, mix well and add the potatoes. Reduce the heat to medium. Use a fork or potato masher, mash the potatoes, mixing them up with the greens. Add salt to taste and serve hot, with a tablespoon of butter in the center.

FISH PEPPER HOT SAUCE

Originating in the Caribbean, it is believed that the fish pepper was brought to the United States by Caribbean immigrants in the late nineteenth century. It grew in popularity in the African American communities of the Chesapeake Bay region, particularly Baltimore and Philadelphia, making the chili pepper a culinary staple in their seafood and shellfish dishes. Long before Old Bay Seasoning spice became popular, the pepper was in common use in many crab and oyster houses, earning it the moniker "fish pepper." It was more of a cooking secret than something well documented. These fish houses typically used the white-hued versions of the chili so that the pepper blended perfectly into cream sauces, keeping the fish pepper low-profile in meals. For the most part, the knowledge of the fish pepper passed down orally from generation to generation.

By the early twentieth century, the fish pepper had nearly become a casualty of the changing times. With few written recipes and an evolving cultural landscape, its use in the region essentially disappeared. It was only in the 1940s that the fish pepper was saved from obscurity. An African American man from Pennsylvania named Horace Pippin, while seeking some bees for an arthritis folk remedy, exchanged a selection of seeds with a beekeeper named H. Ralph Weaver. In the bunch were fish pepper seeds. These seeds stayed in the Weaver private collection until H. Ralph passed down the seeds to his grandson William Woys Weaver, a noted horticulturist and cookbook author. In 1995—nearly a century after losing its popularity— the fish pepper was reintroduced by Weaver to the public. Considered an heirloom variety, the fish pepper has regained some of its original popularity, both as a cooking chili and as an ornamental pepper. Some Mid-Atlantic restaurants, like Woodberry Kitchen in Baltimore, are using it today.

Makes about 1½ cups

¼ cup extra-virgin olive oil
1 small red onion, diced
Pinch cayenne
Coarse sea salt, to taste
1 large clove garlic, peeled and minced

8 to 10 whole fish peppers
4 Roma tomatoes, seeded and roughly chopped
2 teaspoons apple cider vinegar
¼ cup water
¼ teaspoon granulated white sugar

In a saucepan over low heat, warm the oil. Add the onion, cayenne and ½ teaspoon salt and sauté until the onions start to caramelize, about 8 minutes.

Stir in the garlic and fish peppers and sauté for 2 minutes more. Add the tomatoes, vinegar, water and sugar. Mix well and simmer until the mixture begins to thicken, about 5 to 7 minutes.

Transfer all the ingredients to a blender and puree until smooth. Adjust the seasoning with salt to taste. Store the fish pepper sauce in a tightly sealed jar in the refrigerator.

"A WEDDING WITHOUT COOKIES IS LIKE A WEDDING WITHOUT DRINK!": COOKIE TABLES

The cookie table is a wedding tradition deeply rooted in the history of western Pennsylvania, West Virginia and eastern Ohio. In these communities, a wedding without a cookie table is like having a wedding without the bride and groom. Some culinary historians trace cookie or "sweets" tables to European immigrants of Catholic descent—particularly to the industrial areas that employed Italians, Greeks, Slovaks, Serbians, Austrians, Hungarians and Scandinavians who worked in the steel mills, shipyards and coal mines. Others embrace it as a delicious byproduct of America's melting as immigrants strove to assimilate to their new Americanized culture, while retaining some of their Old World traditions. The introduction of cherished recipes for handmade sweets gave both families the opportunity to commingle their cultures with a distinctly personal touch.

In Poland, it was customary for the bride, on her way to be married, to distribute a pine cone–like cookie, symbolizing good luck, to the townsfolk. The traditional Old World Polish wedding included not a cake but a wedding bread of herbs decorated with live flowers. Tables of cookies were also common, featuring chrusciki, Polish tea cookies and assorted rolled cookies filled with nuts, poppyseeds, apricots, apples, plums and gooseberries.

For the most part, the cookie table did not originate in Europe but evolved in America. From 1880 to 1920, immigrants, young men and women, came to this country to find work. Eventually, they met, and subsequently, they married. However, many immigrant families were poor, and their families and church halls were back in the old country, so they devised small home receptions, with a room for dancing and a room for foods and pastries donated by their friends.

Although the beginning of the cookie table in America is debatable, it is the consensus that this sweet sensation has been around since the late 1880s. Every group's introduction to the cookie table differed, but its appeal is infectious. Once encountered, the custom grew in popularity because it offset the cost of purchasing a wedding cake, due in large part to the family and friends who baked for the wedding.

So does it matter where the custom originated, whether the culinary traditions of cookie tables were transported from the old country or whether it was a sweet symbol of the melding of families through intermarriage as mothers, aunts, grandmothers, friends and relatives from both sides of the aisle brought their baked tributes, plain and fancy, to weddings large and small, ethnic and assimilated? If people can appreciate the warm, hearth-and-heart-inspired sense of community and ethnic pride, a time-honored tradition can bring joy and happiness to any gathering, whether a wedding, baby shower, bar or bat mitzvah or christening, with the home-baked expression of love—the humble cookie.

ALMOND COOKIES (AMYGDALOTA)

Although Greeks have accounted for a small percentage of the total immigrants to the United States, they have formed strong ethnic communities that have kept alive their language, traditions and religion. A major unifying force for the Greek community in America was the establishment of Greek Orthodox churches in the United States. Local community organizations called kinotis raised the necessary funds to establish the churches. Many Greeks sought the close-knit communities they had in their home country, and the churches provided the immigrants with forums in which to share their common beliefs, food and celebrations—for example, the simple almond cookie called the amygdalota. These chewy, flourless almond cookies, a traditional treat from the Cyclades islands of Greece, connect Greeks with cheerful moments like weddings. Greeks also believe that their white color brings good luck. Therefore, amygdalota is ideal for Christmas and New Year's desserts. Apart from bringing luck, they are so delicious that you enjoy eating them anytime with no excuses!

Makes about 3 dozen cookies

3 egg whites
1 cup sugar
⅛ teaspoon kosher salt
1 pound finely ground blanched almonds
⅛ teaspoon almond extract
2 tablespoons lemon liqueur or limoncello
30 whole blanched almonds

Heat oven to 325 degrees Fahrenheit.

Put egg whites, ½ tablespoon sugar and half the salt in a medium bowl. Using a hand mixer set on medium speed or a whisk, beat the whites until soft peaks form and set aside.

In a large bowl, combine the ground almonds and extract and the remaining sugar and salt. Fold the egg white mixture into the almond mixture.

Almond cookies. *Natalia Mylova. Adobe Stock Images.*

Wet your hands with the lemon liqueur and divide dough into walnut-size pieces. Working with one dough piece at a time, roll dough between the palms of your hands to form a ball. Transfer dough balls to 2 parchment-lined baking sheets. Flatten each ball slightly by pushing your thumb into the dough to make a dimple. Put 1 almond in the middle of each dimple.

Bake, rotating the baking sheets from top to bottom and front to back halfway through baking, until cookies are pale golden and set, 20 to 25 minutes. The cookies will harden as they cool.

Transfer the baking sheets to 2 cooling racks and let cool. Cookies will keep for 7 days stored at room temperature in an airtight container.

BERGER COOKIES

The history of Berger cookies began in 1835, when German immigrant Henry Berger, a baker by trade, opened his bakery in East Baltimore, Maryland. This thick, soft, vanilla cake–like cookie is similar to the black and whites—also known as half moon cookies—found in the bake shops and delicatessens of New York City. The Berger cookie signature is the topping: a thick and rich fudge-like frosting. This recipe is as close to the original as possible without knowing the secrets that make this iconic cookie.

Makes about 2 dozen cookies

For the cookies:
5⅓ tablespoons unsalted butter
½ teaspoon salt
1 teaspoon vanilla extract
1 teaspoon baking powder
½ cup granulated sugar
1 large egg
1½ cups all-purpose flour
⅓ cup milk

For the fudge icing:
2 cups semisweet chocolate chips
1½ tablespoons Karo light corn syrup
1 teaspoon vanilla extract
¾ cup heavy cream
1½ cups confectioners' sugar, sifted
⅛ teaspoon salt
1 tablespoon sour cream

Preheat the oven to 400 degrees Fahrenheit.
   Line two baking sheets with parchment paper and set aside.

Berger cookies. *Author's collection.*

For the cookies:

In a large mixing bowl, using an electric handheld mixer set on medium speed, beat together the butter, salt, vanilla and baking powder. Next, add the sugar, then the egg, and beat.

Set the hand mixer on low speed and add the flour to the batter and alternately add the milk, followed by the flour, repeating until the milk and flour have been incorporated into the batter.

Using a tablespoon, drop the dough 2½ inches apart onto the prepared baking sheets. Using the bottom of a greased drinking glass, gently flatten each mound of dough to form a circle.

Place the baking sheets in the oven and bake the cookies for about 10 to 11 minutes, or until they're slightly golden brown on the bottom, with barely just a hint of pale color on top. Be careful not to over-bake the cookies. Remove the cookies from the oven and set aside to cool on the baking sheets.

For the icing:

Add the chocolate chips, corn syrup, vanilla and cream to a large saucepan and heat over medium-high heat, stirring often, as the cream will begin to bubble.

Remove the chocolate mixture from the heat and, using a wooden spoon, stir until smooth.

Stir in the confectioners' sugar, salt and sour cream. Set the icing aside and allow it to cool to room temperature.

To ice the cookies, dip the top of each cookie into the warm icing and swirl the cookie to really coat it. Set the cookies back on the baking sheet and repeat the process with the remaining cookies.

Using an offset spatula, spread the remaining icing evenly atop the cookies. Allow the icing to set, then store the cookies airtight in a single layer. Keep at room temperature for at least 3 days. The cookies can be frozen for long-term storage, if desired.

Arnold Reuben

Contrary to popular belief, the first "cheese cake" may have been created four thousand years ago on the Greek island of Samos and not in New York City. In Greece, cheesecake was considered to be a good source of energy, and there is evidence that it was served to athletes during the first Olympic games in 776 BC. Greek brides and grooms were also known to use cheesecake as a wedding cake. When the Romans conquered Greece, the cheesecake recipe was just one spoil of war. The Romans called their cheesecake *libuma*, and they served it on special occasions. Marcus Cato (234–139 BC), a Roman politician in the first century BC, is credited as recording the oldest-known Roman cheesecake recipe. The writer Athenaeus is credited for writing the only known surviving Greek recipe for cheesecake in AD 230. As the Romans expanded their empire, they brought cheesecake recipes to Europe around AD 1000. Great Britain and Eastern Europe began experimenting with ways to put their own unique spin on cheesecake. In Europe, the recipes started taking on different cultural shapes, using ingredients native to each region. A cookbook titled *A Proper Newe Booke of Cokerye* (1545) was printed in London during the Renaissance, and it described cheesecake as a flour-based sweet food.

It was not until the eighteenth century, however, that cheesecake would start to look like something we recognize in the United States today—baked custard with a relatively simple balance of soft cheese, eggs, sugar and a few flavorings, typically atop a cookie or pastry base.

When Europeans immigrated to America, some brought their centuries-old cheesecake recipes along. Many of these recipes fall into four basic types of cheesecake, with the type of cheese being used affecting the texture and taste: curd, such as farmer, pot or cottage cheese; ricotta (Italian cheesecake); quark (German cheesecake); and cream cheese (New York cheesecake). In addition, there is an unbaked chiffon-like version (French cheesecake). Many foods that Americans have come to regard as uniquely "American" are Jewish, originating from the Ashkenazi. Because of the Jewish dietary restrictions (Kashruth), the restriction on serving meat and dairy products at the same meal gave rise to a set of traditional dairy dishes including blintzes, cheesecake and noodle pudding. The concept of delicatessens also came to the United States in the mid-nineteenth century with a new influx of European immigrants. The popularity of delicatessens that specialized in kosher food spread throughout American culture with the help of the Ashkenazi. As delicatessens began to spring up in many Jewish communities, they locally became known as "delis" and proved popular with the general public.

It should be noted that cream cheese has been around since 1872, when William A. Lawrence, a dairyman in Chester, New York, wanted to make an imitation of a neighbor's Neufchatel cheese, a soft, crumbly, unripened cow's milk cheese that originated in 1543 in Neufchatel-en-Bray, France. By 1912, cream cheese had become popular in the Jewish cuisine of New York City, where it is commonly known as a "schmear" and is the basis of the bagel and cream cheese, a common open-faced sandwich sold at Jewish delis throughout New York.

By the 1900s, New Yorkers were in love with cheesecake. Nearly every restaurant had its own version of the dessert on its menu. An early use of cream cheese in cakes was included in the August–September 1909 issue of the *Boston Cooking-School Magazine* as small "Cheese Cakes," instructing, "Press enough Neufchatel or cream cheese through a ricer." "Cream Cheese Pie (Kaeskuchen)" and "Cream Cheese Cake" appeared in 1912 in *The Twentieth Century Book for the Progressive Baker, Confectioner, Ornamenter, and Ice Cream Maker*, published by Fritz Gienandt.

Even though he is best known for his signature deli sandwiches, German immigrant Arnold Reuben (1883–1971) is generally credited for creating the New York–style cheesecake. Throughout his lifetime, Reuben owned a succession of restaurants throughout Manhattan. He opened his first business in 1908 with a delicatessen at 802 Park Avenue and then moved to Broadway and 82nd Street, expanding his deli with a restaurant. There he began serving celebrities and cutting sandwiches with a new twist—on the diagonal. Reuben also claimed to have created in 1914 the famous Reuben sandwich, consisting of rye bread spread with Russian dressing and topped with sauerkraut and slices of corned beef and Swiss cheese, then grilled on both sides.

Thirty years after it first opened its doors, Reuben's Restaurant and Delicatessen finally had a formal opening at 6 East 58th Street off Fifth Avenue with the mayor at the time, Fiorello La Guardia, in attendance. This location was long popular with the theater crowd and celebrities of the day, mainly because it was open twenty-four hours a day. It did its most notable business in the late evening and early morning hours and was known for its impeccable service. Among his regular patrons were Marjorie Rambeau, Gertrude Lawrence, Jeanette MacDonald, Eleanor Roosevelt, the Marx brothers and Eddie Cantor. The after-theater dinner crowd might order one of Reuben's more ambitious sandwiches, which bears his name, or a sandwich named after a show business celebrity, including Groucho Marx, Dean Martin and Frank Sinatra, a gimmick used by many restaurants at the time. Other menu selections include well-known Jewish delicacies such as matzah ball soup and borscht. Reuben's remained in that location until the restaurant was sold in the mid-1960s to Harry L. Gilman and moved to 38th Street and Madison. Marian Burros wrote about the restaurant's appearance on January 11, 1986, in the *New York Times*: "Italian marble, gold-leaf ceiling, lots of walnut paneling and dark red leather seats—to a small-town girl, it was the quintessential New York restaurant." The restaurant later operated at 244 Madison Avenue until 2001, when it was forced to close due to health code infractions.

Arnold Reuben was described as a handsome, blue-eyed man who was always impeccably dressed. The story goes that Reuben was invited to a dinner party in 1929 where the hostess served a cheese pie made with curds. Allegedly, he was so intrigued by this dish that he acquired the recipe from the hostess. He experimented with the recipe. At the time, most bakeries were still using curd cheese or cottage cheese and sour cream as a base for their cheesecakes. By tinkering with the ingredients, Reuben substituted cream cheese for the curds. Reuben's innovation gave the cheesecake its signature creamy texture, and he flavored it with a distinct lemon essence. The graham cracker crust was another one of Reuben's innovations that eventually developed into the beloved New York–style cheesecake.

When Reuben's cheesecake was served plain to high-profile clientele at his restaurants, including the legendary Turf Restaurant at 49th and Broadway in New York City in the 1930s, the dessert quickly became very popular, and it garnered extensive renown and imitation by rival delis. Reuben, who was always widely known as a warm and generous host, also became known as a purveyor of superlative cheesecake. Cream cheese–based versions became the rage of New York City, and New Yorkers have vied for bragging rights for having the original recipe by Reuben ever since.

NEW YORK–STYLE CHEESECAKE

Makes one 9-inch cheesecake

For the crust:
1 ¼ cups graham cracker crumbs
1 tablespoon sugar
½ stick unsalted butter, melted

For the filling:
4 8-ounce packages cream cheese, at room temperature
1 ⅔ cups sugar
¼ cup cornstarch
1 tablespoon pure vanilla extract
2 extra-large eggs
¾ cup heavy whipping cream
Fresh fruit, for garnish

Preheat the oven to 350 degrees Fahrenheit.

To make the crust:
In a large bowl, add the crumbs, sugar and melted butter. Blend until a sandy texture is achieved.

Evenly spoon the crumb mixture into a 9-inch springform pan, halfway up, pressing down the sides and bottom firmly, making the crust adhere to the pan.

Cover with plastic wrap and refrigerate for 15 minutes. Remove from the refrigerator and then bake the crust until set, 10 minutes. Remove from the oven and set aside to cool completely.

To make the filling:
In a large bowl, add 1 package of cream cheese, ⅓ cup of the sugar and the cornstarch together and, using an electric mixer, beat on low until creamy, about 3 minutes, scraping down the bowl several times. Blend in the remaining cream cheese, 1 package at a time, beating well and scraping down the bowl after each.

Increase the mixer speed to medium and beat in the remaining sugar, then the vanilla. Blend in the eggs, one at a time, beating well after each. Beat in the cream just until completely blended.

Gently pour the filling into the prepared crust.

Prepare a bain-marie (water bath). Place the cake pan in a large shallow pan containing hot water that comes approximately 1 inch up the side of the springform pan.

Bake until the edge is light golden brown, the top is a light gold and the center barely jiggles, about 1¼ hours.

Remove the cheesecake from the water bath, transfer to a wire rack and let cool for 2 hours undisturbed. While remaining in the springform pan, cover the cheesecake with plastic wrap and refrigerate overnight, for 24 hours.

On the following day, remove the cheesecake from the refrigerator and unmold from the springform pan. Serve chilled or at room temperature, garnished with fruit if desired.

Cook's Notes:

In slicing the cheesecake, use a sharp straight-edge knife, not a serrated one, to get a clean cut. Be sure to rinse the knife with warm water between slices. Refrigerate any leftover cake, tightly covered, and enjoy within 2 days, or wrap and freeze for up to 1 month.

Index

About the Author

Tangie Holifield is a soil scientist with three decades of experience that have led her to be an advocate for sustainable practices when gathering and bringing it to the table.

As a coauthor of a guide to urban farming distributed by the USDA, she actively promotes sustainable food choices through the recipe selections on her blog, *On the Menu @ Tangie's Kitchen.*

She is also an educator, author, photographer, entrepreneur and culinary enthusiast. When it comes to cooking, she draws inspiration from her family and her global travels. As an experienced home cook, her scientific training has lent an air of precision to her cooking style as she experiments with food to create recipes that are showcased in this latest work. This cookbook hopes to inspire home cooks and food enthusiasts to become more familiar with the origins and modern-day interpretations of food from the Mid-Atlantic.

Please visit her website, www.tangieholifield.com, for current updates on her blogs and forthcoming works.

Visit us at
www.historypress.com